HOUSE IN THE HEBRIDES

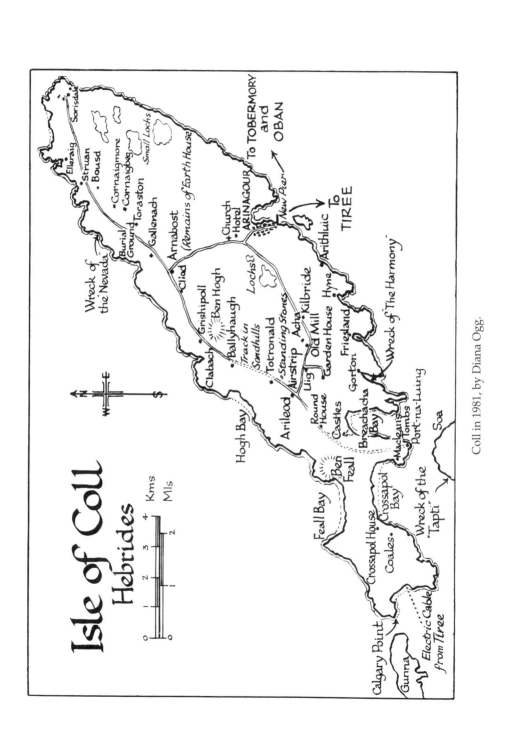

Coll in 1981, by Diana Ogg.

HOUSE IN THE HEBRIDES

JOHN OGG

The waves will beat on the timeless beaches,
the wind will probe and one's problems
will shrink to their true proportions.

John Marchington
The Field
27 June 1968

Cowrie Press
2004

First published in the UK in 2004 by
Cowrie Press
Glencoe, The Ridge, Woodfalls, Salisbury, Wiltshire SP5 2LN

ISBN 0-9548063-0-1

Acknowledgements

Thanks and many thanks are due to:

Diane Fray for typing the initial text.

My daughter Diana, son-in-law Bill and grand-daughter Marion for word processing.

David Bosanquet for his painting and Jim Palmer for his photography.

Mairi Hedderwick for her constant enthusiasm and encouragement in completing this book.

Everyone who has made the Coll experience so special.

I am also grateful to the individuals and publishers who have kindly granted me permission to quote from copyright material, in particular, *The Field* and *The Scottish Field*.

Designed and typeset by Judith Bastin
Printed and bound in Great Britain by Biddles Ltd, King's Lynn

Contents

This book is dedicated to my wife Doreen, who said we could do it. . .
and we did.

Foreword

One of the joys of living on an island is not knowing what the sea will deliver. In the 60's, before cargo containerisation, the sea provided much booty; crates of oranges, tubs of margarine, tins of Klondykers' mackerel, pit props enough to build whole byres and henhouses, driftwood enough for a winter's stove. *Wooden* fishboxes.

And then there was the Eye Surgeon.

As a young family living at Crossapol, at that time, we had to drive along the beach every morning to meet the school van. One day, after a handsome trawl of fishboxes had been jammed into the old Land Rover and Mark handed over to Hughie at the Sandy Hole, we purposefully negotiated the track to Port na Luing to visit the Summer Swallow Eye Surgeon. Mark's little sister, Tammie, had the most attractive, but parentally worrying cast in one eye. The arrival of such a professional on the island was precious jetsam not to be left high and dry on the tideline.

An even more ancient Land Rover was parked outside Port na Luing. Long, oil-streaked shanks stuck out from underneath. The Eye Surgeon's mechanic. We went on up to the fishnet festooned front door; an elegant lady welcomed us. "Is it possible to see Dr Ogg?" we asked, aware, jetsam or not, of our presumption. Dr Ogg would obviously be in his study, after a healthy breakfast of fruits and nuts prettily arranged by his sweet wife, working on an academic tome of eye shattering importance. NOT TO BE DISTURBED.

"He's under the Land Rover", said Doreen.

John disinterred himself, towered over the concerned little family, peered at the toddler and pronounced, "Harmless Epicanthus. A lazy muscle. It'll right itself soon enough. Fancy a dram? Fine fishboxes you have there….."

And so began a friendship that has for ever been linked with drams and fishboxes; quality and staying power being the shared criterion.

A 'fine' box would *never* be used for firewood at Port na Luing. The house was a monument to fishbox furniture. John could transform a functional and sometimes smelly wooden box into a chair, a table, even a sideboard, if winter seas had been generous, each item incorporating the distinctive open handholds.

Bartering a box for a dram – or two – was part of the Port na Luing ritual for me. Crossapol soon boasted its share of fabulous furniture. I write this, on the mainland, 40 years later sitting at a little table with the ubiquitous handles at each side, a bit like a butler's tray on legs; the chair a white-painted specimen of Macintosh proportions, the distinctive handhold panel high above my head. There is a dram on the table.

Part of Port na Luing has floated far from Coll, ever to be celebrated.

Mairi Hedderwick
29 March 2004

1

Invitation to Coll

In the early 1960s, when our fourth child was just a toddler, it was almost a relief to find that we could no longer afford conventional holidays. I have never really enjoyed staying at seaside resorts. I resent having to pay for a swim in the sea and being charged for sitting in a deck chair. I dislike having to queue for a glass of beer and I hate the cacophony of pop music poured out from the transistor radios on the beach. Hotels and boarding houses fill me with remorse. I always eat too much. I have to talk to other 'guests' whose company I do not always appreciate and who probably have no great esteem for mine. Invariably, in the evening the only sitting room is in darkness and dominated by the television.

Holidays abroad are for me one degree worse. I can never understand the language and I am inclined to shout in a silly sort of Pidgin English, which is of course rude and makes me feel very much ashamed of myself. I am an absolute idiot at understanding the currency. I always get excessively exposed to the sun and burn up and itch for weeks. I drink too much of the native wine, which makes me feel awful the next day. I am always terrified that the railways or airlines will go on strike or there will be a flood, an earthquake, or some such disaster and I will be stuck in the wretched place for months and months.

My wife Doreen and I decided that it might be a good idea to find some derelict country cottage, which we could renovate ourselves and use for holidays. Eventually we could perhaps live there permanently. A friend, who was an estate agent, lent me several volumes listing agents up and down the country. The south coast and Cornwall were much too expensive and we did not try the east coast because we felt it would be too cold. We came across a promising little place in Wales, but were let down at the last moment. An approach to practically every estate agent in Scotland failed to provide the sort of place we were looking for. Ruined castles and derelict farms seemed to be in pretty good supply, but no isolated cottages at a price we could afford. Then, quite unexpectedly, a lady, who had once lived in our present house in Hampshire, called on us. She told us that she had retired to an island in the Inner Hebrides called Coll and that her daughter had married the Laird of the island. She thought that in Coll there was a good chance of finding the sort of place we were seeking and invited us to stay with her in two months time.

We had never heard of Coll, nor had any of our friends. We found it inconspicuously marked on a map of the British Isles, about three quarters of the way up on the left hand side. On the scale of our map we reckoned that it was about 12 miles long by three to four miles wide, about two miles from Tiree, eight miles from Ardnamurchan Point on the Scottish mainland, and 46 miles north-west of Oban.

Our local county librarian was most helpful but he too had never heard of Coll. He produced a number of guidebooks, which mentioned the island, but we later discovered that some were inaccurate and clearly had been written by people who had never been there. He found a reference to the Isle of Coll by Betty MacDougall, which gave an excellent description of the island, and we found the translation of Gaelic place names most useful. The earliest description we found was by a Mr Martin Martin, who went there in about 1695. He found that Coll produced more boys than girls and Tiree more girls than boys. We felt thankful that fate seemed to beckon us to Coll and not the sister island when we read further on, 'This isle (Coll) is much more whole-somer than that of Tiree.'[1]

Ryder Haggard was on the island at the end of the 19th century and in *The Farmer's Year* said how much he enjoyed his stay there and how much he liked the people. Murray in his book on the Hebrides likened Coll to Colonsay and remarked, 'Another is the people, a friendly, helpful, smiling people, whom it is good for any man to meet.'[2]

In the *National Geographic Magazine* of April 1961 Captain Allan Villiers described how he sailed his yacht to Coll, 'Coll was the name of a place we liked, a real piece of the Western Islands, unspoiled and unspoilable, despite its loss of population in recent years and the decline of its fishing and agri-culture. It is low and small and off the beaten track.'[3]

Quite obviously Coll had never been much of a tourist attraction. Two of her most distinguished visitors who went there inadvertently were Dr Johnson and his faithful friend, Boswell. In Boswell's *Journal of a Tour to the Hebrides with Samuel Johnson*, he described how they set out from Skye, bound for Mull and Iona, but never got there. Like many sailors before and after them, they found the treacherous seas off Ardnamurchan Point, forced a change of plan. Their small boat tacked hopelessly for Mull and, as the storm increased in fury, they were driven towards Coll. Even the Laird of Coll's son, who was on board, had difficulty piloting the craft into the har-bour. They arrived frightened, seasick and hungry on Sunday 3rd October 1773 and stayed 10 days. Johnson borrowed some books from the Reverend Mr Hector McLean, who was minister of Coll and Tiree, but he soon became bored and said, 'I want to be on the mainland, and go on with existence. This is a waste of life.'

Boswell, on the other hand, seems to have enjoyed himself, and his descrip-tion of the island is worth repeating. 'There are several districts of sandy desert in Col. There are forty eight lochs of fresh water; but many of them are very small – mere pools. About one half of them, however, have trout and eel. There is a great number of horses in the island, mostly of small size. Being overstock, they sell some in Tir-yi, and on the mainland. Their black cattle, which are chiefly rough-haired, are reckoned remarkably good. The climate being very mild in winter, they never put their beasts in any house.

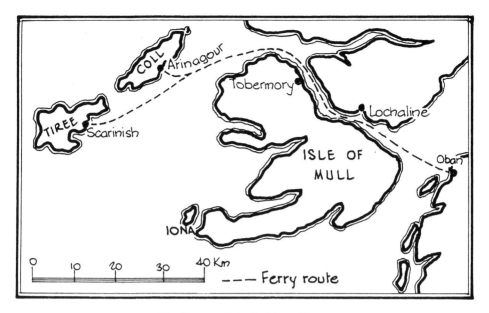

The ferry route to Coll from Oban.

The lakes are never frozen so as to bear a man; and snow never lies above a few hours. They have a good many sheep, which they eat mostly themselves, and sell but a few. They have goats in several places. There are no foxes, no serpents, toads or frogs, nor any venomous creature. They have otters and mice here; but had no rats till lately that an American vessel brought them. There is a rabbit warren on the north-east of the island, belonging to the Duke of Argyle. Young Col intends to get some hares, of which there are none at present. There are no blackcock, muir fowl nor partridges; but there are snipe, wild duck, wild geese, and swans, in winter: wild pigeons, plover and a great number of starlings, of which I shot some and found them pretty good eating. Woodcocks come hither, though there is not a tree on the island. There are no rivers in Col; but only some brooks, in which there is a great variety of fish. In the whole isle there are but three hills, and none of them considerable for a Highland country.'

Boswell's description of the geography, climate and wild life is, we subsequently found, as true today as when he wrote it more than 200 years ago. Some of the lochs have now disappeared and there are no longer any horses, but several ponies and recently donkeys which are increasing in number. Animal husbandry has, of course, changed; the main livestock on the farms is still sheep and there are many beef cattle. The number of dairy cows no longer provides sufficient milk for the island. There are still brown trout in the lochs and 'Young Col' succeeded in introducing hares, of which there are now many. Although there are still no toads or frogs, there are plenty of rats.

Moray McLaren retraced the Hebridean tour in 1954 and in *The Highland Jaunt* had this to say of the island. 'Coll has for the island lover an enchantment all of its own. The highest hill upon it is little over 300 feet. It is about ten miles long: but the flat or undulating road does not go all round by the coast and it would be possible to circumambulate (if one may use so Johnsonian a word) the island easily in one day. The East coast is rocky. The West coast declines to the borders of the Atlantic in some of the most beautiful beaches in all the Hebrides. The celebrated silver and gold of the Western Island sands is here mingled with the very faintest pink colour, which only catches the tail of the eye as you glance at it at first, and then disappears when you look at it steadily. The seas that wash these infinitely delicately coloured bays are, upon a sunny day, peacock-blue and green, dotted here and there with the heads of inquisitive seals. The land between these two coasts is rich, green and potentially fertile, with, only upon the slight uplands, gneiss-rock coming through the surface. Only upon these slight uplands, too, is there heather, and amongst this heather there are tarns and lochans full of eager, active brown trout. Its climate is sunny and peaceful. The great clouds from the Atlantic do not often gather over its flatness, but blow in and onto the mainland and to Mull, to coagulate there and to burst on the mountains. It is an island for dreaming away days of sunshine in Spring or high Summer.'[4]

1   Martin Martin *Description of the Western Isles of Scotland* 1703.
2   W. H. Murray *The Hebrides* Heinemann, London 1969.
3   *National Geographic Magazine* April 1961.
4   Moray Mclaren *The Highland Jaunt* Jarrolds Ltd, 1954.

2

Arrival

A month after reading Moray McLaren's delightful account we set off for Coll. We parked the children, since it was term time, motored up to Carlisle, and then spent the night in Hawick. Next morning we crossed the new Forth Bridge and went over the Grampians and along Glen Coe in pouring rain. It was still raining when we crossed the old railway bridge at Connel.

Doreen and I felt a bit exhausted when we at last reached Oban. It was a Sunday evening. We decided to sleep on the 'Claymore', which was due to sail at seven the following morning. The ship's bar was closed; feeling in need of some liquid refreshment we went into an hotel bar and asked for a half bottle of gin. Quite clearly I had said something awful because my simple request produced an immediate hush. I was told that there was no 'carrying out' of liquor in Scotland on the Sabbath. Another barman gave me a broad wink and nodded his head to a door. I passed through and found a queue of people buying a variety of bottles. All one had to do was to tip the barman and you could 'carry out' what you liked, provided it was adequately concealed. Such were the curious ways in which they used to obey the licensing laws in Scotland.

We were looking forward to sleeping on board ship, but in fact the night was not very successful. The porthole of our cabin appeared to be immediately above the effluent of Oban's main drain. At about three in the morning the town's electricity supply to the ship was cut off. The intermittent noise of the engine room's generator and the clatter of boots on the metal decks put paid to further sleep. We were glad to get up and have breakfast.

It was a bright clear day and by 9.30 am the Claymore was up the Sound of Mull entering Tobermory. Everyone knows when you are entering this delightful harbour because, by the water's edge, is a vertical piece of rock, upon which is painted in large white letters 'God is Love'. Many years ago a child fell from the rocks above and miraculously survived. From time to time the letters are repainted as a perpetual memorial.

On the balcony of the Western Isles Hotel overlooking Tobermory harbour, various people emerged holding cups of coffee and waved to us. We thought they all looked incredibly well dressed for holidaymakers. The hotel is the scene of a weird story told about a skull brought up from the wreck of a vessel of the Spanish Armada lying on the bottom of Tobermory Bay by Lieutenant-Commander Crabb in 1950. The skull was placed in the bar of the Western Isles Hotel. Later someone knocked it over and the same day he fractured his skull in a motorcycle accident. Subsequently a headless body washed up in Chichester Harbour was reputed to be the remains of Crabb.

More recently the proprietor of the Hotel decided to hang up the skull above the bar. He tried to drill a hole in the cranium but the drill broke and the owner immediately suffered excruciating pains in the head.

Coll was another hour away, past Ardnamurchan Point and across the open sea. We had fine views of the islands of Muck, Eigg, Rhum and Canna, with the Cuillins of Skye in the far distance. However our first view of the Island of Coll was forbidding; it looked long, flat and grey, with no sign of human habitation.

The island's only village is Arinagour at the head of Loch Eatharna. At that time there was no pier where the water was deep enough to take the ferry-boat. The passengers and their luggage were bundled through a hole in the ship's side, from whence they leapt into a motor launch. Cattle, provisions, sacks and crates were slung over the side from a boom and lowered into the forward part of the launch.

On our first arrival the sea was calm and the trip to the old jetty uneventful. However on a later holiday we arrived without our luggage as it was too rough to unload it. During a gale the Claymore sometimes missed Coll altogether. In those days Neillie John piloted the launch and John Allen was his mate. It was considerably to their credit that very rarely did anyone fall overboard and luggage was not often lost over the side. Not so long ago cattle were hoisted on to the ferry-boat in a sling. Once, it was told, a fine beastie was swaying several feet above the motor launch, when she decided to lift her tail and do her business on top of the coxswain who happened to be gazing upwards at the critical moment. When the guffaws of laughter had died down, the skipper shouted from the bridge of the ferry-boat, 'My God, Neillie, you were never much of a beauty, but you should see yourself now!'

The arrival of the outward-bound ferry-boat three times a week was something of an event in Arinagour. On this occasion there were quite a number of people on the jetty, including our hostess. After introductions and warm handshakes we went round the village. It could hardly be described as a pretty place. On the left of the road as you looked towards the head of the loch there was a row of whitewashed cottages, a shop and the old smithy, with the school, some council houses and the Free Church manse on the hillside behind. On the other side of the road were several corrugated iron buildings, one of which served as the second shop. Further up the road was the village hall; the doctor's house, the 'Wee Free' chapel and the only petrol pump on the island. On a hill overlooking the village was the hotel and, higher up, was the Church of Scotland. This was a pleasant simple building erected in 1907 but, unfortunately, the magnificent view of the loch and Mull had been obliterated by the use of ground glass in the windows.

Being summer, fuchsias and hydrangeas gave a splash of colour to the village street, which was marred by the number of derelict cars and rubbish on the shore, for which nobody seemed to care or be responsible. Not so the scene at the end of the road leading to the church, for there we found an iron post and part of a rusting gate. The hinges had long since seized up and there was no sign of a fence or a wall. Against the clear sky and the heather covered hillside we could see nothing indecent or melancholic about this useless piece of metal-work; quite naturally it seemed to be just a part of the landscape.

One of the first things I noticed on landing was the absence of police on the island. We sub-sequently discovered that there was no crime; at least none that really mattered. There were very few trees because they were often uprooted in the high winds and there were no television aerials to be seen since there was no mains electricity.

Our hostess pointed out her house, Arivirig, on the other side of the loch and explained that the only way to reach it conveniently was by boat. Accordingly we retraced our steps to the jetty with provisions and a Calor Gas cylinder. All these with our own luggage made a sub-stantial load for the 10-foot rowing boat, which was weighed down still more by a Church of

Neilly John, the ferry master, courtesy of Dave Allan.

Scotland minister who was over on the island for a short time and also stay-ing at Arivirig. The outboard motor started at the first pull of the string and in five minutes we were over on the other side of the loch, unloading every-thing on to the rocks.

The lack of sleep the previous night, a good meal and the smell of the peat burning in the grate had a soporific effect. Doreen and I were both soon asleep. The worries, the rush and the noise of the mainland all seemed very far away. I had a curious dream, in which a Church of Scotland minister kept on prodding me saying, 'There's a gale blowing up. Will you please help me to pull in the boat?' I awoke to find that it was no dream at all, and that it was blowing like blazes outside. A few hours previously the water on the loch had been almost mirror calm but now it was dotted with white horses. We had to lift the boat over the rocks. It took quite a time to get her secure. When we had finished we saw a shallow draught puffer from Glasgow making her way to the pier. She had a jet-black hull and an incred-ibly dirty red funnel well aft. Her hull was down in the water and she was obviously heavily loaded. Every few moments a large wave broke over her and it looked as if she was pitching and rolling like a barrel. The minister told me that she was carrying the year's supply of coal for the entire island and that soon every available vehicle would be down at the pier to collect its fuel. During the evening the wind blew up to gale force and the puffer remained alongside the pier. Later we heard that the skipper and a lad who had just left school were the only crew. In spite of four ropes to the pier she had to run her engine slow ahead throughout the night to keep alongside.

Next morning it was still blowing a gale and I thought it would be pleasant to read by the peat fire. It was not to be. Our hostess announced we were out

Puffer at the pier.

of milk and several other things as well. Since obviously one could not use the boat, she asked me to walk round to the village for the messages. She explained that if I kept by the wall I would find some stepping-stones over the river running into the loch about half a mile away and that there I would be able to join the road. I was given a hiker's knapsack and some empty flagon cider bottles and set off. I did not remember ever having walked in quite such a gale. Great gusts of rain seemed to fly along horizontally and in no time I discovered that my foul-weather clothing was pretty useless. My sou'wester, kept captive with a piece of string under my chin, behaved like a miniature hovercraft. Water squelched out the top of my gumboots. At times I was floundering about in the heather up to my waist. It took nearly an hour to reach the stepping-stones, which turned out to be great boulders across the river. There was no question of walking over them since clearly I would be blown off. I could do nothing but slowly and rather painfully crawl over on my hands and knees. Sometimes during a severe gust I found myself flat on my stomach. Several hours later I returned. I was tired and ached all over but, for the first time for ages, suddenly felt incredibly fit.

The following afternoon the wind dropped and our hostess insisted on taking us over to the village in the boat: we were not very keen on the idea, since it still looked pretty choppy out on the loch, but we got over without mishap, except that the outboard motor would not start, and I had to row.

She produced an elderly van, which had been parked in the village street for several days, and together with the Minister we set off for the east end of the island. There are about 25 miles of roads on Coll: All are single track, with a green ribbon of grass and weeds growing down the centre. Occasional passing places are marked with black and white posts, but we did not need to use them often since there was very little traffic, and the only obstacles were sheep and rabbits.

Many people on Coll never take their cars off the island, and it is, of course, grossly unfair that they must pay the same annual tax as the motorist on the mainland. One can be sympathetic to those who do not bother to pay any tax and disappear with their vehicles when a policeman from Tobermory or Tiree occasionally comes in.

At the petrol pump we took the road to the right and for a mile headed north until we came to a ruined house called Arnabost. This building stands above an ancient earth-house, which gave sanctuary from the invading Norse. We expected to find some sort of cave, but there was nothing to see except a gravel pit, and we were unable to find any sign of an entrance into the ancient dwelling.

After a short distance along the road to the east end of the island we stopped the van to take a look at the new and the very old burial grounds which are side by side, and called the Cillionnaigh cemetery. We were told that many centuries ago a little girl died in a cottage further down the road. Her body was being taken for burial near the village, but an unusual and heavy fall of snow halted the bearers, and she was interred in this place: thus the cemetery began.

The road began to climb and the scenery became grander and more pic-turesque. We came upon one of the only two road signs on the island – the one in the village says 'School' – and this one 'Keep Left': it would really be suicide if one didn't, because on the right is a precipice!

This is one of the 'haunted places' where the 'wee folk' may appear, and very queer things are said to happen. At this place a nurse was once bicycling back in the moonlight from a confinement, and, to her horror she saw a hair-less hare jumping about in the road. Terrified by the creature's pink skin and it's almost human cry, she crouched in panic beside a wall until daybreak.

After passing the farm on the Cornaig Estate we called in at a wee cottage with a black roof, white walls and a red front door, called Struan, where we were welcomed by Mary, who produced numerous cups of tea and hot scones. Years ago she had been a health visitor in Glasgow, but when she re-tired she hardly ever went over to the mainland, and she was always grate-ful to get back to Coll. We found her little house cheerful and spotless, and at one end she showed us a delightful little Free Church chapel, which was once used in the summer months.

Mary arrived in Coll when she was only a few weeks old and left after her schooling. She had come back some years ago with her mother but with nowhere to live. The Wee Free Church offered her her present house, but it was a ruin with no roof. With her own hands she made a wheelbarrow and collected stones with which to repair the walls. She had few carpentry tools and when she had to make a hole in the remaining timber she used a red-hot poker.

At the back of the house there used to stand a blacksmith's shop but years ago wind-blown sand covered it up and on the site of the smithy Mary kept her hens. It was here that we saw a remarkable sight – a tied up sack that was lurching about like something out of an animated film. Mary explained that it simply contained a broody hen and, after a few days in such uncom-fortable confinement, it would soon learn to lay again!

On the other side of the road we called on Morag, a very elderly lady who had spent a simple and contented life in one of the few thatched houses on the island. She told us how, in her younger days, she had pushed her fist through the roof: She found a square foot of glass which wedged nicely into the thatch, and when the sun was in the right direction she was able to read. A while later she did the same thing on the other side. She found that she could read for most of the day.

Morag's mother knew the secret of dyeing wool with wild flowers, lichens and various vegetables. She also made primitive crockery by heating a pile of limpet shells in the fire until they turned grey and became brittle. These could then be ground up into a powder to form, with milk, a sort of cement, which was fashioned into pots and glazed in boiling milk. I was told that some of her pots still exist on the island but I have never seen any of them. It was here we saw one of the four letter boxes on the island. It was so primitive I had to make a quick sketch of it!

It was getting near suppertime, so we put off seeing Sorisdale at the eastern tip of the island, and returned to the village. It began to rain again, and returning to Arivirig in the boat we saw a magnificent rainbow over the house.

Next morning I tried my hand at stacking peats, which had recently been dug from behind the house, but it was not easy, and each time I made a little pile they were blown over. I gave up, and tried casting a wet fly in one of the little lochs beyond the peats. I was told that the water was full of trout, but I never saw a rise and caught nothing. I remembered how once I was with a Royal Marine Commando, who got a splendid bag of fish by throwing a hand grenade into a Welsh river! (Much later I discovered that the only way I could catch Coll trout was with a spinner or worms!).

After lunch Doreen and I got a lift to Acha, which lies in about the centre of the island. Here there was once a school, but the Laird, his wife Janet and their family then occupied it. Janet told us there were still people on the Island who once went to the School in Acha. Few of the pupils had shoes and they usually remained unshod until their first job at the age of 12. All year round every child had to bring a piece of peat to school: anyone who didn't had to sit at the back of the class and shiver.

A stream runs through their garden from the Mill Lochs further inland, and in the old days it used to turn the waterwheel of the mill, where the meal was ground. It was then a derelict, pleasant ruin, with a few trees growing in a patch of ground, which used to be the yard. It was sad to reflect that it was many a year since any wheat was ground on Coll, and now the bread is imported from the mainland – much of it tasteless, deathly-white processed chemical stuff which is nothing more than a vehicle for butter and marmalade or jam.

From Acha we borrowed a couple of bicycles and took the road to Arileod; this was the farmhouse of Alec and Flora, who were later to become close friends. A little further on we reached the Round House which is square in shape, but once upon a time there did stand a round observation tower at this site: When it was burned down the stones were used to make the existing cottages. We then came to Breachacha Farm. There, before the last war, was one of the centres of the Coll cheese industry, which in it's day

The Bousd letterbox.

was a flourishing concern, and produced nearly 100 tons of cheese a year, some of which, it is reputed, was always on the menu in the House of Commons dining-room. With the onset of war production ceased and the industry has never been revived. Many of the cheese presses are still intact and could probably be made to work again.

Near the farm we saw men planting potatoes. In a corner of the field was a pile of daffodil bulbs which had been cleared . . . rather a sad reminder of a daffodil industry on Coll and Tiree. The Dutch bulbs grew well and produced splendid flowers, but the stems were perhaps a little too short. Sadly, harvesting, packing and transporting were not cost-effective and the project, after a few years, failed.

We pushed our bicycles through the back gate of Breachacha Farm, which led into Breachacha Field, 'the dappled field', so called because in the summer it is a mass of wild flowers, including orchids, which grow almost down to the water's edge of the bay. Breachacha is well known for its ancient castle. Archaeologists, used to spend their summer holidays sleeping under canvas in the field while making excavations, and described it as a small but most perfect example of a medieval stronghold in the Hebrides, and it would seem likely that it was designed by an exceptionally skilled architect, and put up by expert masons. It stands only a few hundred yards from the sea, and was once, probably, surrounded by a moat filled with salt water.

The keep, with its seven-feet thick walls, stands in the centre of several smaller outbuildings and once contained a basement and four floors. The windows are very small, and it must have been a pretty dark place inside. Its first occupant was Angus Og, Lord of the Isles and a friend of Robert the Bruce.

In about 1750 the old castle was abandoned, and Hector, Uncle of 'Young Col', who was so kind to Johnson and Boswell, put up a mansion a stone's throw away, known as the New Castle. While we found the old ruin picturesque and delightful, the new looked a bit grotesque. It consisted of a central square block with a wing fanning out either side for the servants and the stables. Johnson, as always, was forthright in his opinion, and said to Boswell: 'There was nothing becoming a chief about it: it was a mere tradesman's box.' When we first saw it, it had been empty for nearly a quarter of a century, and was in a pretty derelict state, because a few years previously some lunatic had destroyed some of the windows with slugs from an air gun. In no time the wind and the rain, the ravens and the starlings had produced utter chaos inside. The floor of the library was rotten with fungus, and covered with damp, disintegrating books; wallpaper flapped in the wind, copper piping was green with verdigris, birds-nests seemed to be everywhere, and the whole place had an air of melancholy and gloom.

We were glad to get into the fresh air again and to cycle westwards from the dappled field. On reaching the North Strand we had a look at Feall Bay. Here we found a mile or more of lovely sand with the uninhibited Atlantic rollers roaring in. At the far end of the bay, round a headland, we were able to see Barra and the Outer Isles.

From Feall it did not take long to push the bicycles over the sand hills to Crossapol Bay. The sea was much calmer here and again we found over a mile of sand without another soul in sight. We tried cycling along the firmer sand at the high water mark, but soon got stuck and had to push the machines. At the south-western end of the bay we took a look at the MacLean's tomb, where Alexander, the 15th Chief, was buried in 1835 together with his wife and a friend. It was a horrid little example of thoroughly bad architecture, uncared for and falling to pieces.

On our way back to Acha we left the road and walked down to a small house called Gorton on the west coast. There we were told was a fine brass bedstead, which was reputed to have been the one that Johnson slept in when staying at the New Castle. Unfortunately no one was at home but we could just make out the outline of a fine bed through one of the windows. Of more interest to me were the remains of an ingenious horse driven threshing machine, which was still in quite a good state of preservation. It consisted of a 12-foot metal bar mounted horizontally; on one end a horse was harnessed and the other end was fixed to a cogwheel, which was connected by a shaft to the threshing machine. The machinery was kept in motion by the horse walking round in a circle.

Maclean's tomb at Crossapol.

Doreen seems to have relations all over the place. It wasn't much surprise to find her cousins Ken and Bea Cassells in the village. Their house was a relatively modern one next to the Hotel. Bea used to make all sorts of things on her sewing machine, which she sold at the gift shop in the village. Ken wore a very ancient kilt. He was a botanist and had created a superb garden. He was also an expert on whippet hounds, being a well-known judge who was much in demand. He had also written a book about these animals.

After four days we had seen about half the island and much of what we had seen we had liked very much indeed. We had found a small, depopulated but cheerful place containing sky-blue lochs and fringed with magnificent beaches. We had had many fine views of the Outer Isles. The weather had been mild and exhilarating to the point that a strong wind could almost knock one over. We had found a very friendly, unostentatious, naturally inquisitive, almost classless society, for which time seemed to mean little or nothing at all. Our only disappointment was that we had been unable to find a house. The only building we had been shown was the empty Church Manse, which was much too big and expensive.

We had planned to return to the mainland and motor up to Ullapool for the remaining week of the holiday but our hostess insisted that we stay for the installation of the new Church of Scotland Minister, who was to replace the locum staying at Arivirig. We were bidden to the village hall at 8 pm but we later discovered that this was about the time you were supposed to leave your home, as the show did not begin for another hour. The retiring Minister began making a speech but the diesel electric generator promptly failed and the lights went out. Undismayed he continued by lamplight. There followed a speech by the new Minister, and then a Moderator of the Church of Scotland rose to his feet. The packed audience was expecting some pretty heavy pronouncements, but instead he told a story about a

Church of Scotland Minister and a 'Wee Free' Minister from Coll who were out in a boat fishing on Loch Eatharna. A Catholic Priest from one of the outer islands joined them. After a while the Church of Scotland Minister got out of the boat, walked over the sea to the hotel, and came back with a tray of refreshments. A little while later the Wee Free Minister repeated the performance. Greatly impressed the visiting Catholic Priest got out of the boat with the tray and promptly sank to the bottom of the loch. He had to be hauled back into the boat by his companions. Full of apologies he tried again but the result was the same. The Wee Free Minister glanced at his Church of Scotland colleague and said, 'Do you think we ought to show him where the stepping stones are?' The islands are either Catholic or entirely non-Catholic; Coll is the latter and I have since heard this story told with ministers of different denominations.

More speeches followed, presentations were made, and the children put on a splendid show of Scottish dancing. Alastair, the landlord of the hotel, played his concertina as well as performing a first class magic act. (He was a member of the International Brotherhood of Magicians.) In the early hours of the morning we went to bed only to get up again at 6 am to say farewell to the departing Ministers. It was raining hard. Neillie John was loading the motor launch. With a wicked grin he came up to the Moderator and myself to ask us to give him a hand. For the next half-hour we carried empty ice-cream containers, drills, and broken agricultural equipment down the slippery steps. At last, with a cheery smile, the Ministers waved goodbye as the motorboat disappeared into the mist.

We left two days later. However we were invited back, with our children, the following August. Somewhere in that lovely island we were sure must be the house that we had been seeking for so long.

3

We Find Port na Luing

When August came and we were back at Arivirig we had the feeling that we had never been away. On every subsequent visit to the island we have always felt the same. We were enormously happy to find that our children, Dorothy Anne, Diana, David and Stephen, enjoyed Coll as much as we. The rowing boat, the ponies for the girls, gorgeous August weather, and those wonderful beaches with their Atlantic rollers set the stage for a perfect family holiday.

In the village we were able to hire a very ancient saloon car, which we called 'the Wreck'. When it worked it went extremely well, but it was temperamental and sometimes did not function at all. There was one particular switch on the dashboard, which caused black smoke to pour forth from under the bonnet whenever it was turned on. It was intriguing to watch the windscreen wipers go on working long after everything had been turned off.

We often went over to Haugh and Feall Bays. We swam, slept in the sun, ate picnics, and collected seashells and oval stones polished by countless tides. At that time we found on the beaches glass fish net floats, which have now been replaced by aluminium or plastic balls. In fact we thoroughly enjoyed ourselves but all the time Doreen and I still felt that somewhere in that lovely island must be the house, which we were searching for.

With only two days of the holiday left I began to feel desperate. Janet, I think, sensed my despair and quite nonchalantly suggested that we might care to take a look at a house called Port na Luing. However she did not think that it would be any good at all, since it was so isolated and such a ruin.

She thought that long ago, a ferryman who rowed people over to Tiree had lived there. He also refreshed them with strong ale brewed on the premises. The last occupants were the MacLean family who left in about 1935. She was told that he was a cobbler who felt the cold terribly and so did his work in front of the fire, with his coat fastened up with an enormous safety pin. His wife was a kindly soul who kept open house for any visitor. By all accounts she was reputed to have been something of a soothsayer. At the Coll show she put up a wee tent and would tell your future in return for a coin. Janet went on to explain that the door of the house had to be removed a few years previously after a cow got in, the door closed, and the animal died of starvation. As far as she knew the place was built in about 1760.

We had been told that the house was only about a quarter of a mile to the south of the MacLean's tomb at Crossapol Bay, but in fact we had quite a job

Port na Luing as we found it.

finding it. We felt it unwise to push our luck too far with the Wreck and left it parked at the end of the road a little way beyond the Round House. We walked over the sand hills and searched for nearly an hour. Then quite suddenly from the top of a hill we saw below us the ruined house called Port na Luing right on the edge of the Atlantic between two outcrops of rock.

It was a lovely afternoon. The sky and the sea were perfectly blue. The fields were a mass of orchids and other wild flowers. From the doorway of the house we could see Mull beyond the little islands of Soa and the Treshnish group. In the far distance we could also see the Paps of Jura. A few hundred yards in front was an old jetty, once used for exporting barley to the Campbeltown distilleries and off-loading the coal frigates. The end of the pier had been destroyed by an exceptionally heavy gale. It was also obvious that the entrance of the little harbour had been silted up so much that at high water it was only a few feet deep. However it was obvious that it could have provided first-rate shelter for a small boat.

In the little bay in front of the house several grey seals popped up and down looking curiously at us. The only sounds were those of the sea and the birds. We fell in love with the place at once. It seemed idyllic being a perfect retreat for holidays and perhaps one day for retirement. However there were snags. The nearest house was two miles away and the rough track was often impassable by car.

The croft had been empty for a very long time and was knee-deep in cow manure, guano, old lobster creels, and disintegrating fish boxes. Nothing was left of the window frames, much of the timber was rotten, and a quarter of a century of gales had played havoc with the slated roof. We had been told that occasionally an exceptionally high tide came in through the door. Moreover everyone in Coll said that Port na Luing was haunted.

We knew that we would be unable to employ anyone on the island to rebuild the ruin and to have imported contractors would have been

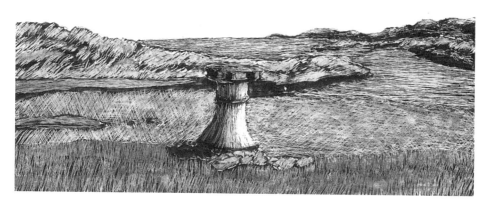

The old capstan at Port na Luing.

prohibitively costly. The only people who could rebuild the croft must be ourselves, and any friends we might persuade to join us. Furthermore, it would be impossible to obtain any building material in Coll. Everything from flooring joists to the smallest screw or nail would have to come from the mainland. Neither Doreen nor I knew the first thing about building.

As we lay in bed that night in Arivirig some eight miles away, it seemed to me that the prospect of rebuilding Port na Luing was just a pleasant pipe dream. I disliked climbing ladders. My experience with hand tools was very limited. My cloistered hospital occupation and lack of exercise had made me physically quite unsuited for such a crazy venture. I told Doreen that the whole thing was off but, to my amazement, she violently disagreed with me. She argued that to work on the croft would be a splendid way of spending holidays! After all, our home was only 572 miles away. We could easily get in timber by cargo boat from Glasgow. We could have a roof rack put on top of the car. If other people had learned how to rebuild houses why couldn't we? As to cost, she would simply have to manage with less housekeeping money and we could both give up something. To improve my health I could take the dog for long walks every evening. With these illogical arguments running through my mind, I fell asleep.

Next day we revisited Port na Luing. The weather, as so often happens on Coll, had changed overnight. A gale was blowing from the south-west and the front of the ruin was wet with sea spray. It began to rain and water poured in through the gaping holes in the roof. We climbed over the rubbish in the back and hundreds of starlings flew out of the window. Loose slates groaned in the wind so that it was easy to understand how the house had a reputation for being haunted.

In the sunshine of the previous day the thought of rebuilding had seemed daunting enough but in that gale the prospect was for me utterly hopeless.

Doreen remained convinced that we could do it and she produced all the old arguments and many more. In truth, she was much more farsighted than I. As she stood there, drenched to the skin, she was already planning our future home. To satisfy her I made some preliminary measurements. Outside the house was 40 by 18 feet and the granite walls were more than two feet thick. We could not get up to the roofing beams but we estimated that if we were to replace the old joists and to make an upstairs floor with dormer windows, the latter would have to be about four feet wide. Later we discovered that the true measurement was 50 inches.

That night we had dinner with Janet and the Laird. Just before we left I casually asked him if he would sell us Port na Luing with some ground. To my utter dismay he said that he would sell me the house and an acre of ground for £150. So the deal was clinched.

Early next morning we left the Wreck near the jetty. As Neillie John piloted the motor launch out to the ferry-boat we could see that the old car's wind-screen wipers were still working. 'She's not waving goodbye,' exclaimed Doreen, 'she's calling us back.'

4

Training and Planning

Doreen and the children said that I should go to keep fit classes but I would not for one moment entertain the idea. Instead I bought some strong shoes and started walking. My first effort was just under four miles. I came home limping and absolutely exhausted. I was reminded of the time when, another flat-footed temporary probationer Surgeon-Lieutenant RNVR and myself were appointed to a Royal Marine Commando training school in Wales. To our horror we were sent on an endurance march. We spent hours staggering about in bogs on some awful mountain. When eventually we reached a road, we were picked up by a fish van and given a lift back to the camp. We hid in a drainpipe under the road until we were certain that the last man had got back and then tottered into the mess to celebrate our achievement.

However, I persevered with my walking and eventually thoroughly enjoyed it. My record was 14 miles but it took me a whole Sunday to achieve this.

I discovered that I was very much overweight so I spent much of the winter of 1964 on a diet consisting of little more than water with a little bit of lean meat and salad in the evening. I think I might have faded away altogether if the hospital pathologist had not asked me if I was suffering from consumption or some other wasting disease. Taking a look at myself I realised that I was becoming emaciated. I took Doreen out to dinner and got through about 3000 calories. It was fun to be eating again!

If I was going to shift hundredweight bags of cement and heave flooring joists into position, I obviously had to do something about my arm and chest muscles, so I went round to the local sports shop. A giggling girl assistant sold me a pair of dumbbells and wrapped them up in a paper bag. On the walk home one fell out with a frightful clatter. I felt that everyone was laughing at me as I retrieved the wretched thing from the gutter. I blushed like a beetroot and rushed on. We had fun with those dumbbells; my elder boy, David, and I had competitions to see who could hold them above our heads the longest. We also lay on the floor and did press-up exercises. However I began to ache terribly and gave them up.

I hoped that the do-it-yourself magazines might tell me how to rebuild my ruin. I bought lots of them and was greatly impressed with their multi-coloured covers, which always seemed to depict a youthful, smiling, good-looking couple, immaculately dressed, performing such tasks as installing a central heating system, building a kitchen extension, or converting the attic into a cocktail bar or viewing lounge. Alas, the contents were not of much help to me. Having read such articles as 'Building a Swimming Pool', 'Making a Dog Kennel', and 'How to rewire the Electric Kettle', I decided that I must turn elsewhere for inspiration and instruction. We read everything we could about the Hebrides. In one book nearly an entire page was devoted to Port na Luing and how it was haunted, and how no Collach would dare go down there after sundown. We found nothing specifically relating to the rebuilding of ruined crofts but gained some degree of comfort from Gavin Maxwell's *Ring of Bright Water*. Although his ill-fated house, Camusfeàrna, was further away from the sea and would seem to have been in much better structural condition than Port na Luing, he obviously had to contend with formidable transportation problems. We were impressed to find that he had made furniture from driftwood and old fish boxes. I was determined that I would try to do the same.

I got hold of a book on carpentry but on the first page was told that no amount of theoretical knowledge was any substitute for practical joinery. I signed on for evening classes with the local College of Further Education. All the other pupils were at least half my age and obviously very experienced. I was given a set of tools and a bench, which had clearly been designed for use by a child. Bent double I did my best to construct joints but they were either so tight that they split terribly when I tried to hammer one bit into another or so loose that the two members jangled about like a semaphore arm. No amount of glue would persuade them to unite at a right angle. Eventually I tried to make a chair. I was so ashamed of the thing that I never brought it home.

I became rather depressed, but my friend, Roy, told me that he thought I was wasting my time learning joinery and all that would be necessary at Port na Luing would be rough carpentry. He knew of a cottage, which was being modernised and was quite sure that the men working there would give us some tips. The following Saturday Roy, his wife Bunny, Doreen and I went along to a pleasant little cottage on the banks of the Hampshire Avon. We explained our problems to the foreman who, without hesitation, took us upstairs to show us how a dormer window was being installed. The thatch had already been removed and a beam cut away in the roof. On top of the exposed wall a piece of wood, called a 'sleeper', had been cemented into position. On to this we watched the wooden window frame being secured. Next two triangular pieces of one-inch thick chipboard were cut out and secured by means of screws to each side of the wooden window frame. Then a sort of lid, which was also made of chipboard, was fixed over the aperture above. We took note of their tools and they kindly gave us samples of the various types of screws and nails they were using.

With the lesson still fresh in our minds we immediately returned home and made plans. We knew that the width of the dormer windows at Port na Luing must be approximately four feet wide so we took the plunge and ordered three of them from the local timber merchant. When they arrived they were already covered with pink priming paint. We added two coats of white undercoat and three of topcoat.

No jetsam is wasted. Driftwood barrel seat (above left) and table (above right).

Roy and Bunny were getting interested in Port na Luing. Having recently had a lot of experience in rebuilding their own cottage, they would obviously be just the people to help us with our own project. We asked them if they would come up to Coll during the following Easter holiday. Without a moment's hesitation they accepted. We celebrated with another 3000 calorie meal.

By frankly admitting my utter ignorance of building techniques, I very soon found that the experts were only too willing to tell me all they could. One of the hospital plasterers took me aside and gave me half an hour's instruction in plastering and mixing cement and concrete. His mate enthusiastically put me through a sort of crash course in drains and drainpipe laying. The store man in a builders' yard let me look round his stock. Here were nails and screws of every conceivable type and gauge for me to see and handle. There were also hinges, guttering, plumbing materials, paints and brushes. In fact everything and much more, that I could ever possibly require.

I had rather a vague idea that quite early on in our building programme I would have to install water pipes and piping for bottled gas. Another friend, also called Roy, had at one time served in the Pioneer Corps and was an expert in plumbing. He showed me how all the cold water supply and drainage could be quite easily carried out in alkathene piping, but that I would have to use copper for the hot water and gas supplies. He showed me how to bend an elbow in a copper pipe without producing a nasty kink. The trick was to push a metal spring into the pipe before slowly bending it over your knee. Having got the required angle the spring was extracted. He warned me of the risk of copper sulphate decomposition in a salty atmosphere and how I must clean all the piping with wire wool and paint it after the final installation. He also showed me how to bend alkathene in boiling water, how certain connectors and T pieces for copper piping required no solder, how to fit a tap washer, and many other things.

With yet another friend I spent a pleasant weekend at his holiday cottage in Cornwall. This had just been put on to mains electricity. I helped strip out the gas piping. He very kindly presented me with his old Calor gas refrigerator and yards of piping and fittings. We went through the catalogues and wrote to Calum, the gas agent on Coll, for a cooker. Since the manufacturers were giving a 10 per cent cut on all their products for one month only, we rather recklessly, ordered a gas water heater as well.

We estimated that eventually we would have to put 15 window frames in Port na Luing. Since it was unlikely that I would be able to obtain glass cut to the correct size on the island, I decided that I would have to cut it myself. Unfortunately my efforts were disastrous. I put on goggles and heavy gardening gloves and scratched the glass with a wheel cutter making a deafening screech. I turned my head away, ground my teeth and clenched my fists trying to bend the pane along the incision. Of course, the glass shattered into a hundred splinters. Undismayed I obtained 30 sheets properly cut to the correct size and packed them between newspapers into a crate that just fitted into the boot of the car. Later that crate travelled to Oban, was loaded onto the ferry-boat, was transferred to the launch, was hoisted onto the jetty, travelled on the roof of the Wreck to Breachacha, and finally reached Port na Luing in a trailer towed by a tractor. Not a single sheet was broken. If I couldn't cut glass, at least I could pack the stuff!

Our original plan was to make a central hall leading into a bathroom behind. A single staircase would lead from the hall to the centre of three interconnected bedrooms upstairs. On the right of the hall would be the sitting room (later to be known as the drawing room), and on the left the kitchen. Roy persuaded us that a staircase in the hall would take up a great deal of room and that we would require every square inch of hanging space for clothes. He suggested that we should make two staircases, one going from the kitchen and one from the drawing room. In this way friends could go up and downstairs at any time without passing through our bedroom and two staircases were obviously better than one in the event of a fire.

We produced plans as accurately as we could on squared paper but discovered that children's Lego building blocks made a nice three-dimensional model, which was pretty much to scale. It was from this that we finally made our measurements for timber. We ordered 20 flooring joists 16 feet by six inches by four inches; 100 tongued and grooved flooring planks, and also a number of runs of four by two and two by one inch timber. In addition I asked the timber merchant to send over 12 sheets of eight by four foot chipboard. It was important that all this should not be left lying about on the pier exposed to the spring gales, and so we asked the Glasgow timber merchants to despatch our order six days before we arrived on Easter Monday, 1966.

As to hand tools, I realised that it was absolute folly to buy anything but the best. Cheap tools would not last, would behave badly, and could be dangerous. I was fortunate in having an interesting set of carpentry things, which had belonged to my late father David Ogg. Historians remember him as an authority on Europe in the 17th century; I remember him for his quiet unassuming manner, his almost perpetual consumption of frightful pipe tobacco which gave off acrid fumes that my mother declared rotted the curtains; his love for an ancient Oliver typewriter upon which he would bang away with two fingers until the early hours. In particular I remember him for his appreciation of fine woods and veneers and for his painstaking inlay work, which transformed awful old furniture into things of beauty. From him, to a small degree, I inherited his love for certain crafts and the ability to use my hands to make things. Admittedly the sessions at the carpentry classes had been disastrous, but I was nervous and much too tall to work at such a diminutive bench. I discovered that to pursue a craft I must work alone and develop unorthodox techniques, which suited my particular temperament.

My father's box of tools was clearly not enough and there would be other skills besides carpentry, which we would all have to understand. I knew something about plumbing but was still pretty ignorant of masonry work and tiling. Much later we discovered that we had to learn a little about electrical installation, brewing, baking and navigation.

From an organisation with the impressive title of 'The Country Gentlemen's Association' we ordered a wheelbarrow, ladder, spade, shovel, a fork, cross-cut saws, hammers, setsquares, screwdrivers, rulers, tenon saws, hand drills, a set of chisels, and a spirit level. In addition we obtained a mallet, plane, clout hammer, cold chisels, wrecking bar, plastering tools, spanners, a hack saw and other things for metal work. Finally we put all the tools on the sitting room floor at home. They looked rather like the list of bone instruments that a newly appointed Orthopaedic surgeon would submit to the appropriate committee! Roy took a long searching look and then said, 'There's only one thing missing from here and that's a whip!' An ironmonger in Oban supplied a workbench, six sacks of cement, 28 pounds of assorted nails, four rolls of roofing felt and 12 gallons of various paints. We felt well equipped for the tasks ahead.

Everyone was provided with a complete set of foul-weather clothing. Doreen insisted that all of us, including the children, were measured up for boiler suits. These proved to be the most practical working garments. Clothing was packed into one trunk and the tools into another. We sent them off by train six weeks before the date of our arrival since British Rail had such a bad reputation for delay. To give credit where it is due, our entire luggage arrived on Coll within a fortnight of despatch and never at any time subsequently did we experience any trouble in sending trunks and packing cases to Scotland.

At last the great moment arrived. Roy and Bunny set off with the two girls and the personal luggage in their car. We drove the two boys and Cherie, our mother's help. On the roof of the car we carried the three window frames and in the boot a chemical closet, coils of alkathene, copper pipe and fittings, and the crate of glass. I promised the children that we would see snow before teatime. In fact they had their first glimpse of it at Kendal, where we stopped for a picnic lunch outside a factory which made snuff.

I felt that it was important that the first night should be as comfortable as possible since I reckoned that there would be some pretty hard living during the coming fortnight. We put up at a delightful hotel near Moffat but arrived there three hours earlier than expected. We learned our first lesson, that travelling to Scotland by the motor roads was incredibly fast. Before long it became faster still so that then we often no longer stopped for the night but motored straight through from Fordingbridge in Hampshire to Oban in about 11 hours. Not any more. There are now too many cars – ours is one of them. The frequency and frustration of delays has taken the pleasure out of motorway driving.

The following day was a Sunday and it was snowing hard. We missed the turning for the Erskine Ferry, but got through Glasgow with very little difficulty. The trip through the snow-covered countryside by Loch Lomond was breathtakingly beautiful. We wondered why anyone ever wanted to go abroad for their holidays. Since then we have seen the loch in every mood. Sometimes the sunshine has been so bright and the colours so vivid as to be almost blinding. We have seen the water covered with a mist and the islands on the loch seemed to be floating in the air. One night we saw the lights of Alexandra reflected by the clouds on the surface of the water. Once we had a glimpse of a snow covered Ben Lomond in the moonlight. In June the rhododendrons by the water's edge are a beautiful sight.

There were several inches of snow at Oban and it was bitterly cold. We were all glad to have a hot meal and to get on board the Claymore. The children had never slept on board a boat before and there was the inevitable altercation as to who should occupy the top bunk. We tucked them up and, with much reluctance, I said goodbye since I had to attend a meeting in Edinburgh the following day. I spent the night at an hotel near the pier. Next morning I saw the ferry-boat steaming out towards Lismore Island as I walked to the station to catch the early train and to travel by what was left of the once proud Caledonian Line.

5

The Work Begins

It was snowing hard when I returned to Oban from Edinburgh two days later. I wondered what the weather was like 58 miles away on Coll. I had a clue from a telephone message which was waiting for me at the hotel. It was from Doreen; cryptic and to the point, it simply said, 'Bring rugs'. I ordered four but was rather taken aback when I was asked what tartan I favoured. I said, 'MacGregor', since the Aberdeen brethren of my family were in some way connected with that clan.

The snow was still falling when the ferry-boat left, though by the time it reached Tobermory the sun was shining, but it was still very cold. As the launch approached the jetty on Coll I searched for some of my family, but to my disappointment nobody was there. The Wreck, however, was in its usual place. In spite of the intense cold it started at once.

I met Doreen and Bunny several miles away at Acha Farm walking towards the village. They hadn't worn a watch or seen a clock since they arrived and thought it was an hour earlier and that they would have plenty of time to hitchhike into the village. Already the relative unimportance of time on that little island was taking effect. Both of them looked very happy and incredibly fit, but it was evident that neither had had a decent wash since they left the ferry-boat. I was, of course, eager to know how they had been getting on at Port na Luing, but they told me that it was to be a surprise, refusing to tell me anything.

We got the Wreck a short way beyond Breachacha. As we walked over the hill I saw a great cloud of smoke coming from a bonfire behind the house. In front there was a monumental pile of manure and rubbish. Roy and the children looked even dirtier than the wives, but our youngest, Stephen, was the dirtiest of them all. He never had much time for washing and this was seventh heaven for him! Suddenly they all began talking at once. I gave the children a box of Edinburgh rock, which kept them quiet for a moment. Roy explained how they had found all the crates and trunks in the barn at Breachacha Farm. They set off pushing a trunk in the wheelbarrow and carrying as much as they could. They had not gone far when Jimmy, the Laird's foreman spotted them. He had loaded everything into a trailer and towed it down by tractor. (Later we were to discover that this was the first of his many kindnesses to us.)

They showed me a mountain of timber, which had been brought down by Calum, the Calor Gas agent, in his lorry and which he had stacked nicely outside at one end of the house. Inside a dramatic transformation had taken place since I had been there seven months previously. Every scrap of manure was now outside. The old beams looked smaller without their pile of guano. They were disappointed, they explained, to have found rotten timber in the floor of the kitchen and the hall. However in the drawing room they had unearthed a concrete surface.

We sat down on some crates and had a picnic lunch. I told them about my trip to Edinburgh and the lavish reception and cocktail party; of the wonderful views one saw as the train meandered along the banks of Loch Awe; and how on the way back I had seen two deer silhouetted against the moonlight. David suggested that it might be a good idea if I stopped blathering and got on with some work. I took the hint, put on my boiler suit and boots, collected some water from the burn, and made up a solution of strong disinfectant.

The smell of the antiseptic reminded me of the hospital. As we scrubbed the floor and walls, wood lice appeared from everywhere. I had never seen so many nor such magnificent specimens. Treatment of the walls produced a rich harvest of creepy things of every sort and description. Next we removed the flooring joists; they came out without much trouble. They were made of Scotch pine and in some, one could see the original carpenter's adze marks. Many of them were still in good condition except at the ends where they had lodged in the recesses in the wall and gone rotten. As soon as a beam was removed Cherie and the children would climb up and remove any old birds' nests and other things from the wall recesses, and chuck the rubbish on to the bonfire. All the new timber was carried in. Before we left that night we lit some DDT cones, which put paid to the remaining bugs.

During that holiday we stayed at an interesting wooden bungalow near the castles on the shores of Breachacha Bay called Stronvar. It had been built early in the 20th century as a sort of overflow for guests at the New Castle. With children in mind, the architect had made the corridors about eight feet wide, and the bedrooms were like cells in a honeycomb – excellent, our children discovered, for hide and seek. At times it had also functioned as a shooting lodge. We were interested to see in a 1915 tourist's guide to Scotland for sportsmen that there were then about 14,000 acres of shooting in Coll and that the bag could include about 80 brace grouse, 200 brace partridges, 600 snipe, 150 woodcock, 30 geese, 150 hares, and a good many rabbits (black), besides duck, teal, plover, etc. It was not made clear how long it would take the sportsmen to inflict this phenomenal slaughter, but we felt it unlikely that he would obtain such a bag in just one day of shooting. The same guide explained that there was an excellent nine-hole golf course in the immediate vicinity of the castles, but this has now completely disappeared without trace.

On the walk along the seashore from Port na Luing to the bungalow, Doreen told me that the puffer with coal had not yet made its yearly visit and that all the fuel had now been used up. We gathered every scrap of driftwood we could find, but in spite of the large fire the bungalow was bitterly cold. We stuffed towels into the gaps under the doors. Everyone had a hot water bottle and an extra rug. I don't think that one of us took off anything more than our shoes when we went to bed that night.

Next morning we awoke with phenomenal appetites but had to wait awhile for breakfast. Because the old gas cooker was due for replacement it took nearly 20 minutes to boil the kettle and we never managed to make any toast. We had plumbing problems too since it had not been possible to renew the ancient pipes during the previous winter. While Doreen and Bunny were preparing breakfast, the rest of us queued up to take turns pumping cold water into a tank in the attic. The amount of water in the tank was indicated by a bit of lead on the end of a piece of string attached over a pulley to a float on the surface of the water. As we pumped away so the lead weight very slowly moved down the wall passing the 'empty', 'half', and 'full' marks. Some visitor with a sense of humour had written 'FLOOD' in large letters below the 'full' mark.

We reckoned that we must work the pump handle back and forth 84 times on each occasion that anyone pulled the chain in the bathroom. We were warned never to allow the tank to become empty, but with nine people in the bungalow it very soon did and an airlock formed. Our younger daughter, Diana, who was always the first to spot any disaster, rushed into the kitchen and announced that no cold water was coming out of the taps but the hot was running beautifully. At the same moment Cherie, almost in tears, told us that she had a terrible pain in her stomach and was feeling sick.

While Roy shovelled out the burning timbers from the boiler, I had a look at Cherie and found that she had a 'Coll tummy'. This is a mild but quite unpleasant form of enteritis, which affects many newcomers to Coll. It is supposed to be due to drinking infected water. I told her that she must stay in bed for 24 hours. During the first day of her illness Doreen looked after her while the rest of us continued work at Port na Luing. As we left with our rucksacks filled with sandwiches and thermos flasks, Doreen announced that she would clear the airlock and have hot baths for us all when we returned in the evening. According to Cherie, Doreen spent most of the day banging all the cold water pipes with her fists and was quite exhausted by the time she had expelled the last air bubble and got the water flowing again. We all had baths that night, but by the time it got to my turn the water was luke-warm so I didn't stay in for long.

Next day Cherie was quite herself again and we celebrated her recovery with a trip to the cinema. At that time the show in the village hall took place once a fortnight provided the weather allowed the ferry-boat to get in with the film and that the electric generator functioned. News of the entertainment appeared as a notice in MacDonald's shop window but there was no guarantee that the film shown was the one advertised as sometimes the wrong one arrived. This, of course, added a little speculation to the performance. On the night the hall was packed for a James Bond film. Adults paid three shillings and the children one and sixpence. The hire of the film and the cost of the projector were heavily subsidised. Willie, the shepherd, wrote out the advertisement beforehand, took down half a dozen people from the west end of the island in his van, got the generator going, collected the cash and projected the film. We enjoyed the show enormously including a two-month old news film. Our only criticism was that the sound from the two loudspeakers was absolutely terrific and would, we felt sure, have been adequate for the Albert Hall.

The film was so good that we soon forgot about the hard benches. Since there was only one projector, Willie turned on the lights between each roll of film so that he could see to thread on the next. These interludes enabled some of the audience to refresh themselves with a wee dram from their hip-pocket flasks. In later holidays the girls used to go to the cinema by themselves, have a lift back to Breachacha Farm with Willie, and then walk the one and a half miles down to Port na Luing, getting back at about midnight. Once, on a dark night, Diana tripped over a hedgehog and both she and Dorothy Anne fell over a sleeping cow. They were livid that I hadn't picked them up, but we wondered where else in the British Isles our daughters could walk that distance in the dead of night and come to no more harm that falling over a hedgehog and a cow.

In a few days we were packing in as much physical work as would occupy us for a month or more at home. We all slept incredibly well and after a while hardly ever tired during the day. Very soon we all felt extremely fit. The freedom from worry, which I have always found at Port na Luing, is, I believe, linked with the utter unimportance of time there.

Whatever else we did that holiday it was essential that we made a part of the roof as watertight as possible. We had already decided that wherever we found a bad hole we would put in a dormer window. In this way we could keep out the rain and let in the light. In fact this unorthodox plan worked extremely well as we ended up with five dormer windows pretty symmetrically placed. To put in the windows we required a working platform. There was no question of erecting scaffolding outside the house because we didn't have any. It seemed that the obvious thing to do was to replace the old joists and lay a part of the upstairs floor first.

Replacing the old joists proved to be quite a job. Most of the beams sent over from Glasgow were slightly too long and our muscles were not yet in training for sawing rapidly through such large pieces of timber. To get each beam perfectly level and of exactly the same height, it was necessary to jack up one end with pieces of broken slate, or in some cases, to chip away bits of granite to form the bases of the retaining slots. As soon as a beam was seated to our satisfaction, the space left in the slot on either side and above the beam was plugged with cement. Sand was readily available a few yards away on the seashore, but we soon discovered that it was quite hopeless to try and make a cement mix on boards out of doors since the wind blew away most of the cement powder. With the wheelbarrow in the drawing room it was a simple matter to make up small quantities of a mix at a time. Later I was told that one should never make cement from seashore sand; we must have been lucky in some way because our sand made excellent cement and has never given us any trouble.

It was while we were putting in the joists that we noticed Stephen, who was then six years old, was missing. We found him in the kitchen sheltering from the rain under a polythene bag. He was soaked and shivering, but he soon recovered when we took off his wet boiler suit, wrapped him up in rug and gave him some hot coffee. This incident made me realise the importance of giving everyone a specific job to do. Stephen was presented with a broom, dustpan and brush. From then onwards, when he wasn't playing on the beach, he was almost constantly occupied sweeping up the mess that accompanied practically every job.

Once the joists were in position, the tongued and grooved flooring boards went down pretty quickly. The children laid flat on the floor, which had already been laid and pulled on each plank so that its tongue firmly jammed into the groove of its fellow. The adults hammered the plank on to the underlying joists. We found that the flat types of nail were much easier to use than the round varieties and less liable to split the wood. At first we often bent nails before they were hammered home but, when we slowed down the work proceeded much more smoothly.

By the end of the fifth day we felt pleased with our progress. The old house had been cleaned out and disinfected, rotten timber had been burnt, about half of the old flooring joists had been removed and replaced, and the floor of two of the upstairs bedrooms had been completed. Unlike some builders we had heard about, we had remembered to leave a gap in the floor for the staircase from the drawing room.

It was time to pause and have a party. Doreen and Bunny produced a splendid meal. We bought bottles of wine and whisky from the hotel. By constantly stoking the fire and bringing in a paraffin stove we succeeded in establishing quite a fug in the bungalow. Jimmy and Margaret, who lived nearby, came to dinner. Jimmy was quite a small man who had spent most of his life on the island. He had a soft delightful voice and sometimes spoke in the Gaelic. After the meal and a few drams we persuaded him to give us his party piece, which was a recitation of 'MacAlister'. I have heard him recite this poem on many occasions since, but never grown tired of it. It goes like this:

> Clansmen, the peats are burning bright,
> Sit round them in a ring,
> And I will tell of that great night I danced before the King.
>
> For as a dancer in my youth
> So great was my renown,
> The King himself invited me to visit London Town.
>
> My grand new presentation kilt
> And ornaments I wore,
> And with my skean-dhu I rapped upon the palace door.
>
> And then I heard a lord or duke
> Come running down the stair,
> And to the keyhole put his mouth demanding 'Who was there?'

'Open the door', I sternly cried,
'As quickly as you can –
Is this the way that you receive a Highland Gentleman?'

The door was opened, word went round,
'MacAlister is here!'
And at the news the Palace rang with one tremendous cheer.

The lovely ladies of the court
with pearls and jewels all decked,
They blushed and trembled as I bowed to them with great respect.

Slowly at first with hands on hips
I danced with ease and grace,
Then raised my hands above my head and swifter grew my pace.

At last no human eye could see
My steps so light and quick,
And from the floor great clouds of dust came rising fast and thick.

The King was greatly moved
and shook my hand in friendship true.
'Alas,' he said, 'although a King I cannot dance like you.'

And then the gracious Queen herself
Came shyly o'er to me,
And pinned a medal on my breast for everyone to see.

A whisper I shall ne'er forget,
Nor how her eyes grew dim,
'Ach, where were you MacAlister, the day I married him?'

We started work next morning on the roof. In addition to the very large hole in the bedroom, the ridge was sagging badly. Very slowly we removed the old beams and pushed up the ridge with a piece of four by two. A frightful rattling began as more slates fell off and we were covered with bits of old birds' nests and other rubbish. Eventually, with some almighty heaves, we got our ramrod into the vertical position and wedged the bottom end into the bedroom floor. However the floor began to sag perceptibly with the additional weight of the roof. After some rapid measurements a second piece of four by two was erected from the concrete floor of the drawing room to the floor above. In this way continuous support was given to the roof 20 feet above the concrete floor. The lower beam later made an excellent side for the staircase. With the ridge at last straight, new roofing beams were soon nailed into position.

We had brought with us several gallons of wood preservative solution. The accompanying blurb had assured us in glowing terms and superlatives that when liberally applied it would not only eradicate any established rot, but would prevent any wood decay developing. We filled up four jam jars and sent the children up inside the roof, where, sitting astride the tie beams, they applied the fluid with considerable vigour. Soon everything, including ourselves, became stained a bright green. We began to choke and our eyes smarted terribly. It was quite evident that nothing could survive that toxic vapour. This was the first of several occasions when we were to be driven out of the house by fumes or smoke.

Putting in the dormer windows necessitated removal of one of the roofing beams. In our first effort we were rather anxious lest the lack of support would cause part of the roof to come crashing down on top of us. The beam running down the centre of the great hole looked pretty rotten, having been exposed for a number of years. However, after sawing for a short way we met stiff resistance finding that most of the wood was rock hard. No movement occurred in the roof and work proceeded almost exactly as we had been shown in the cottage by the River Avon during the previous autumn. We placed the top on to the dormer frame and nailed the felt into position just before a gale blew up and the rain came hurtling through. We quickly pinned some polythene over the window apertures but, with the force of the wind, the sheeting was either torn away or the drawing pins were shot out like bullets. Our newly laid floor was getting soaked and the water was dripping through into the drawing room. There was nothing else for it but to put in the glass at once.

This was my first attempt at glazing and I shall not quickly forget it. On top of the ladder the wind seemed ferocious. In spite of foul-weather clothing the rain lost no time in getting down my neck and running down my arms. It was difficult to get the putty to stick to the wet frames and my fingers became numb with cold. When I climbed the ladder again with a mouthful of glazing tacks, a hammer under one arm and a sheet of glass under the other, I felt quite sure that I would be blown away. On the other hand, I was much more concerned about the glass than about my own safety. Eventually the panes were securely home. It was nearly dark but already the bedroom seemed much warmer. That night we heard on the wireless the weather report for coastal waters. In sea areas Malin and Hebrides it was blowing a gale of force 9 to 10 on the Beaufort scale. The next morning the ferry-boat bound for Tiree did not attempt to get into Coll.

By lunch time the wind had eased a bit and we decided to take the afternoon off. We motored over to the eastern tip of the island where once several hundred people had lived in a village called Sorisdale. Only three brothers lived there then. Their cottage was roofed with thatch held down with a giant hair-net like contrivance made of wire netting and stones. Several of the ruined crofts remained but most were completely derelict with fuchsias growing through the walls. A few had been converted into cattle byres.

Two of the brothers were twins. The older man, Neil, was the cook and housekeeper. He was a delightful character with a tremendous sense of humour. 'Don't you ever get lonely down here?' Roy asked. 'Not at all. We get the local news on the telephone and hear what goes on elsewhere on the wireless. We get the Oban Times wrapped round the bread.' He paused. 'It's a week late but it makes no difference, the news is always the same anyway.'

We watched one of the twins manuring a field. He put his tractor into low gear and then climbed into the trailer, chucking out the seaweed as it slowly moved along. Near the end of the field he clambered back onto the tractor, turned it round, and then got back into the trailer and carried on manuring.

From the top of the hill behind the brothers' house one could usually see Eigg, Rum, Muck and the Scottish mainland. A short distance beyond the hill lies one of the finest bays on Coll. Although the sun was shining the wind was bitterly cold. Never the less the children insisted on having a swim; I think David stayed in for about five minutes. Later we heard that on that day the road to our house in Hampshire had been impassable because of snow.

On the way back we were in time to telephone the ironmonger in Oban for some rolls of fibreglass to insulate the inside of the roof. In the bar of the hotel everyone was eager to know how we were getting on. Although they were very encouraging, it was evident that they all regarded us as crazy.

The glass wool arrived two days later. Together, with the groceries, it filled the back of the Wreck so several rolls had to be tied on to the roof. At Breachacha the boys with the wheelbarrow joined us. Between us we tried to get the stuff down to Port na Luing. However on many of the rolls the outer wrapping had come adrift in transit and very soon it began to blow about all over the place. We lost some but managed to retrieve most of it, together with a fair amount of sheep's wool, from the barbed wire fence that ran beside the track. Our efforts were not in vain as many people have since remarked that Port na Luing is one of the warmest houses on Coll.

The second dormer went in much more easily than the first and the glazing presented no particular problems. We lined the chipboard roof and walls of each dormer with the glass wool insulation, and then covered the wool with planking. By the time we had made the wide windowsill, the bedroom was beginning to look pretty good. The ladies climbed the inside ladder with a thermos flask and some biscuits; we put up deck chairs and for the first time in about 30 years a meal was had in Port na Luing in comfort. This was also the first occasion that we had all been able to sit down and enjoy the view. Until then none of us had noticed that Ben More on Mull was covered with snow. It was a scene that has never since lost its charm.

Naturally, like everyone else on the island with a house overlooking the sea, we claimed to have the best view. The truth is that whenever you can see the sea through your windows everything is interesting and constantly changing. The mood of the sea is never the same. Sometimes, but not often at Port na Luing, there was a mirror calm. Within hours a gale or a mist would blow over Mull and Soa. There were always birds around and in every sort of weather the seals came into our little bay. Sometimes otters were about. In the summer we saw up to a dozen basking sharks gliding through the water. Occasionally we have seen the glistening black dorsal fin of a killer whale, which broke the surface to blow from time to time. Most days we saw ships and sometimes unexpectedly a yacht or the lobster boat from Tiree. Once we thought we saw a Polaris submarine on the surface.

View of the house and Soa from the hill behind the house, known affectionately as Ben Ogg.

At dusk and during the night the view is different but just as beautiful. In June we sometimes see the fireworks display of the aurora borealis in the northern skies. In a gale our lights might serve as a homing beacon for hundreds of sea birds, which fly a few feet above the waves towards the house, rising up and just clearing the roof before veering off to the west. The moon and its reflection on the sea take on an ever-changing pattern. This is all the more unpredictable as clouds in turn eclipse the reflection. In high summer it never quite becomes dark and to the north at midnight in June it is always light. Shooting stars seem larger than in the South of England. Unless there is a mist we can see the lights of the Roan Bogha Buoy, which marks the half way position on an east–west course from our harbour to Scarinish on Tiree.

Most visitors agreed that our view was the finest on Coll. A few other houses have a view almost as good but the perfection of some is spoilt. Other buildings, caravans or man made pollutants get in the way. We had none of these at Port na Luing. In any sort of weather if you felt bored you only had to look out of the window! We have never felt the need for a television.

To our great regret Roy and Bunny had to leave us. For the remaining few days of our holiday there were times when we felt very isolated and some-times rather lonely. There was still plenty to do since the roof over the bed-room was by no means watertight. By standing on the roof of the dormer I could quite easily replace many of the missing slates. My ladder, however, was not long enough to reach the damaged area around the ridge and the lead capping was split in several places. I had not at that time discovered that it is easy to make a roof ladder by tying a piece of wood at right angles to one end of the ladder and slipping it over the ridge. Instead I tied a large brush on to the end of a pole, dipped it into bitumen, and began to slap the thick paint over the damaged area. I soon discovered that I could only reach out far enough by tying a rope around my shoulders. When the other end was secured through the window to a beam in the bedroom I was able to lean outwards at an angle. This Heath Robinson method enabled me to complete the immediate job. However it was only temporarily successful as much of the paint was eventually washed away. Years were to pass before I thought that I had made the roof safe and watertight and able to stand up to the force of any gale.

On the last day of our holiday we made a door out of chipboard, fixed a lock, and screwed on a nameplate, which I had made from the top of an old piano. In my ignorance I painted upon it a ling fish in blue and the name of the house in red. Several years later I discovered that Port na Luing was an abbreviation for Port-na-Luinge-Bahte, meaning Port of the Long Boat. We took an inventory, boarded up the downstairs windows, lit some more DDT cones, and very reluctantly returned to the mainland.

6

The Seamen's Strike

When we got back home we began making plans for our return visit in the following June. We had taken photographs of every stage of the rebuilding and a later study of the projected transparencies helped us considerably to plan the next phase. A camera with a flashbulb attachment served us well. It was not until several years later that we allowed ourselves the luxury of a telescopic lens for bird photography. Roy produced an eight millimetre cine camera and subsequently showed us a most interesting film. In the general chaos of unloading everything from the cars at Oban, he put a film, which he had just exposed back into the camera again, and so doubly exposed everything. He could not have animated it better if he had tried and we were entertained with views of seagulls sitting on the horns of highland bulls, the ferry-boat floating through a ploughed field, and a lighthouse perched on top of the old castle at Breachacha.

The one chore, which I disliked intensely during our early days at Port na Luing, was emptying the chemical toilet. In a caravan, where it would serve perhaps just two or three people, I imagined that there would be no great problem. However in our house it had been in daily use by nine, and no more need be said. We could not consider any sort of conventional closet because it seemed very unlikely that we would ever have enough water. We had seen an advertisement for a mechanism wherein a pint of chemical solution would effectively cope with the situation. When full one pulled a lever, which caused the sterile contents to disappear down a pipe into a soak-away. We ordered one and, although it was not possible to install it until the following year, it proved a tremendous success.

Another matter that was causing us some concern was the fact that very soon our entire family, and possibly friends, would be living at Port na Luing. With so much building work ahead of us we would have to provide more room for storage. One of the widely advertised extra rooms was the sort of thing that we had in mind. Although they looked well and gave excellent service on the mainland, the only one that had been put in Coll had been badly damaged by the first gale. Back at home we eventually made a frame for a porch, which measured 10 feet by eight feet, in four by two inch timber. By this time I could make fairly good joints and the frame stood up on the lawn without glue or nails. Each piece was numbered, taken down, tied up in bundles and sent to Oban. We later put up the porch in two days and nailed it to the crevices between the granite walls with dozens of six-inch nails. It has proved a tremendous success not only for storage but also as a pleasant place to sit and have a meal. It stops the south-westerly winds from blowing into the house. In February of 1968 the wind velocity on the Tiree weather station 12 miles away was recorded as 120 miles per hour. (We were told that in fact the wind blew even stronger than this; the true force was never registered because the measuring instrument was blown off the mast.) Margaret wrote and told us: 'The air was full of porches and hen coops flying about'. She did not exaggerate as we found that the Acha Farm barn had blown across the road and demolished the telephone wires to Tiree. However our porch, which had been exposed to the full force of that terrible gale, had come through unscathed.

The walk from Breachacha made a pleasant break in the day's work when the weather was fine, but it was an unpleasant and tedious business pushing down the groceries and other things in the wheelbarrow in a high wind and driving rain. We had no guarantee that we would always be able to hire the Wreck. What we really wanted was a four-wheel drive vehicle that would take us all the way down to Port na Luing. Eventually we discovered one of the early models of the short wheelbase Land Rover. The canvas roof had seen better days, the body was a bit dented and needed repainting, but the man in the garage assured me that it was mechanically in good condition and so I bought it.

I had never driven a car of this sort before. I was quite amazed how it would travel over the most appalling terrain with no trouble at all. I drove it to work and with fiendish delight left it in the car park outside the hospital next to a Rolls Royce belonging to one of my more affluent colleagues. After a few days I had absolute confidence in the machine. Doreen and I decided to drive it up to the Glasgow Docks and to have it shipped over in time for our next holiday. This also provided us with the opportunity of taking up a number of things, which would otherwise have had to go by rail.

Along one side of the Land Rover we stowed a folded double bed with the mattress on the floor. Two four-foot long asbestos chimney pipes fitted nicely onto each of the back seats. Each pipe was stuffed with blankets. Three 50-gallon plastic water tanks nested into one another took up most of the remaining room. However we discovered that by taking off the canvas roof the refrigerator, without its legs, would slip into the top water tank. Obviously the refrigerator could not go up empty. Having packed a hurricane lamp into it there was still quite a lot of room left. I felt that it was a good idea to get together a collection of books so that anyone staying at Port na Luing would find something of interest to read. In forming the nucleus of my Coll library I felt rather like the people on the BBC's Desert Island Disc programme, who were severely limited in their choice of gramophone records and had to concentrate on quality rather than quantity. Quite by chance my first three were all by authors from the western hemisphere: the *Complete Works of O Henry*, several novels by Stephen Leacock, and Thoreau's *Walden's Pond*. The last was one of the most delightful books that I have ever read. Trollope's autobiography, little read today, was wrapped up with Thoreau. There followed Murray's excellent *Guide to the Hebrides*,

Alasdair Alpin MacGregor's *The Western Isles*, Eric Linklater's *Prince and the Heather*, Gavin Maxwell's book about otters *Ring of Bright Water*, Rutley's books on mineralogy and sea fishing, and from the now defunct New Naturalist Series, *Natural History in the Highlands and Islands* by Fraser Darling and other volumes. Doreen somehow found space for several bird books in one end of an asbestos pipe.

Thus loaded, the machine, with its bulging canvas sides and the refrigerator making a prominence in the roof, looked rather like a portly old gentleman wearing a top hat. The orifice in the back flap, which had once served as a window, gaped more widely than ever giving rather a melancholy appearance to anyone approaching

The Land Rover Limo.

the vehicle from the rear. In sheer devilment I drove the Land Rover to the hospital again and parked next to the Rolls Royce. Next morning we left at six o'clock but we could not travel faster than about 40 miles an hour. At this sedate pace it was possible to enjoy the scenery. By Carlisle the posture produced by the bucket seat was beginning to do curious things to my back and I had to make frequent stops for a stretch and a brief walk. We were soon lost in Glasgow but were tremendously impressed by the efforts everyone made to try to show us the way to the docks. Perhaps we looked rather pathetic, but I am quite sure that some of those kind people would have climbed in and personally directed us, if there had been room. At Glasgow Central Station we caught a sleeper back to London. Both of us were asleep before the train left and did not wake up until we reached Euston.

On the following day the seamen went on strike. Some pessimists predicted that everything would be pinched from the Land Rover in Glasgow Docks, but much later we discovered that not a thing went missing. The Prime Minister solemnly addressed the nation and told us that no good would come out of the strike. In fact, after weeks of negotiation the men of the British Merchant Navy were promised better pay and conditions. Having on occasion seen the crew's quarters in various merchant ships, my sympathy was largely on the side of the seamen. Our Mercantile Marine was justly honoured and praised in time of war, but with peace it had been sadly neglected by successive governments.

The crew of the Claymore were on strike. The only vessels running a regular service to the Hebrides were frigates of the Royal Navy and they were taking just essential supplies. We wondered how on earth we would be able to get to Coll from the mainland. We telephoned Alastair at the hotel who cheerfully told us that we would have no trouble at all. We would be able to get to Grass Point on Mull in a motor launch from Oban. A bus would take us on to Tobermory where Guy would pick us up in his yacht. Because of the strike there were few visitors to Coll and we would be able to hire the Wreck again.

The Oban dock was reminiscent of the day I had called in there on board an armed motor fishing vessel during the war. We found corvettes and a minesweeper moored alongside the deserted ferry. The streets seemed full of sailors. I had a chat with one of the ship's officers and explained that I had a crate of crockery, a window frame, a few gallons of paint and a couple of rolls of foam rubber mattresses which I would be grateful if he could take to Coll. He was sympathetic but adamant that, under no circumstances, could they carry anything but food. I think he must have felt a bit sorry for us because he insisted on buying Doreen and myself a drink!

At dawn on the following day we clambered into a motor-launch, which was already pretty well filled with passengers, mailbags, and provisions for Mull. The skipper was a lady of indeterminate age, who continually smoked a cigarette whilst piloting her craft with the nonchalance of a nurse pushing a pram.

It was dead low water at Grass Point on Mull. The top of the jetty was about 12 feet above the gunwales of the launch. An elderly gentleman was sitting on a packing case; we were asked to help him aboard since he was on his way to hospital on the mainland and unable to climb down the rocks. It was evident that he was in a fairly advanced stage of heart failure and it took some time to lower him into the boat. Eventually we had him comfortably seated under some tarpaulin. A man on the jetty helped us to unload our belongings and we passed up crates of bread and groceries. He turned out to be the local grocer and gave us a lift to the bus stop.

It was still early in the day when we arrived at Tobermory so we took a walk to Ardmore Point. There is a lighthouse there, which was unattended and automatic. The deserted keepers' cottages were in a fine state of re-pair and would have made a good home for someone who did not mind the isolation. The tide was going out. We watched the oystercatchers peck-ing limpets off the rocks. We never discovered if these delightful birds could really open bivalve oyster shells in the same way, although we have read that they eat mussels. On the way back we noted a not unpleasant smell, which we could not identify at first. Then we realised that it was garlic. There were, in fact, hundreds of wild garlic plants growing alongside the path. A Scottish 'Hramsa' soft cream cheese contains highland wild garlic and herbs, and very good it is too.

We found Guy at Tobermory buying provisions. He explained that there were five other passengers for Coll but they were unlikely to turn up for a while since the pubs were still open. In fact, they seemed to stay open for most of the afternoon and it was after four o'clock by the time we set off. The evening was blisteringly hot without a breath of wind. The yacht's auxiliary motor had seen better days so it took nearly four hours to get to Coll. Guy cursed our slow progress but for us it was a splendid beginning to our holiday. We had never been so close to the coast of the island before. We saw several basking sharks and dolphins, and also gannets, guillemots, cormorants and other sea birds.

The ferry entered Eatharna Bay to the west of a wee island, but Guy manoeuvred his yacht through a narrow gap between the east of the little island and Coll. He told us that once upon a time on a Hogmanay morning the ferry approached the bay full speed ahead. On sighting the motor launch the skipper rang down to the engine room to stop the engine. However the engine room crew were unconscious after their celebrations and the boat began heading at maximum speed for the hotel at the head of the loch. With considerable presence of mind the skipper steamed hard to starboard and back into the sea through the narrow gap, which we were just entering. Apparently the

Guy Jardine, courtesy of Mairi Hedderwick.

ferry-boat suffered very little damage but we gathered that some of the engine room crew were replaced. (A good story, but personally, I don't believe it!)

Dinner that night with Janet and the Laird at Acha was a most welcome affair. The seamen's strike was becoming a confounded nuisance they explained, as they could not replace broken equipment or ship livestock to the mainland. At the best of times farming on Coll had its frustrations and difficulties. It was evident that the recent and unexpected impositions were hard to bear. They had plenty of food apart from bread; indeed, with the dearth of visitors, the two shops had never been so well stocked.

It never really gets dark on Coll in June. Although it was nearly midnight before we parked the Wreck at Breachacha, we found that by the time we arrived at Port na Luing we did not need a light. The house seemed to be much as we had left it but we were really too tired to do anything more than unroll our foam rubber mattresses onto the bedroom floor and turn in. To describe them as mattresses might be an injustice to those thick soft contrivances that cover the springs of an average bed. Ours were no more than an inch thick being perhaps one degree softer than sleeping on the bare floor boards. (I only once slept on a harder bed and that was at Owen's Park Undergraduate Residence in Manchester University.) However we were really too tired to worry much about personal comfort and were soon asleep.

At about four in the morning a sort of dawn chorus of sea birds suddenly awoke us. The noise occurring in the absolute silence was quite terrifying. It sounded as if every gull for miles around was engaged in mortal combat on our rooftop. The din kept us awake for nearly an hour.

The absence of most sounds except natural ones is one of the features of
Port na Luing, which all our visitors very soon notice. On the mainland one
accepts a great deal of mechanical background noise, which usually passes
unnoticed, but in our house one only hears the sound of the sea and the
birds. Sometimes, when the wind is in the right direction, the noise of a
ship's diesel engine far out in the Sound of Mull can also be heard. We very
soon got to know the particular throb of the ferry's engine as she passed us
early in the morning on alternate days and the sound would sometimes
awaken us.

The gas cooker had arrived before the strike. Calum and his wife, Janet,
brought it down in his lorry. Fitting it up was not difficult. It looked very
fine in the corner of the drawing room with its rack full of plates. The book
of directions made quite entertaining reading; it even pointed out that once
a kettle was boiling, however much longer you went on boiling it the water
didn't get any hotter. Doreen lit each burner in turn with a separate match
thrilled to see that the thing really worked. Janet reprimanded her and said,
'Anyone can see that you're no' an islander. When your last box of matches
is finished you'll have to travel eight miles for another.'

We put a T piece into the reduction valve and were able to mount a lamp
over the cooker and one in the bedroom upstairs. Calum also brought down
a table from Acha Farm. This had spent a long time in the hen yard but
looked very presentable when cleaned. With the same load came a whatnot
from Alastair. It was both ornamental and useful unless one leant on it,
whereupon the top shelf would crash down on the one below with a dreadful clatter. We always referred to it as a dumb waiter.

Without Roy and Bunny we did not feel very confident about putting in
the third dormer window. However, once we had removed the slates and
reached the point of no return, we had the framework up in a day and completed the job the following morning. The woodwork in the second bedroom
was a slow business because we had to put in a partition wall to form a
corridor. Doreen's approach to carpentry was unorthodox but effective; she
regarded the timber rather as if it was material for a dress but instead of
cutting it out with scissors she used a saw.

We lived very well on powdered milk, some eggs and a ham. We baked
our own bread. After five days though we began to feel rather lonely and
went into the village. In the shop I bought a mirror and was quite startled to
see how dreadful I looked with a week's growth of beard. I then understood
what an elderly and much respected highlander in the hotel bar meant when
a few minutes before he had said, 'It's awful easy to go native in these parts.'
One thing pleased me in the shop; our groceries were labelled not 'Mrs Ogg'
but 'Mistress Port na Luing'. I felt that perhaps we were beginning to be
accepted as part of the scene.

We met Janet and the Laird in the village. Doreen cheerfully invited them
to dinner at Port na Luing the following evening. I pointed out to Doreen
that we had no window in the drawing room and only a few deck chairs.
She disregarded these trivialities and began preparing the meal. I had only

The drawing room window with a view of Soa and the
Atlantic.

one window frame and that was earmarked for the fourth dormer. However
by cutting off one end I obtained an excellent fit in the drawing room
window. I had it glazed and painted and found time to make benches out of
flooring boards before our guests arrived.

The dinner party was a tremendous success. Afterwards we climbed the
ladder to the bedroom, had a glass of beer and sat looking at a rainbow over
Soa. We were all rather quiet for a while and then the Laird said, 'If anyone
had told me two months ago that I would be having dinner in Port na Luing
tonight, I would have said that he was crazy.' We felt rather proud.

A day before the end of our holiday we had used up all the wood. Since it
was a fine day we packed some sandwiches and took a walk towards Gunna
at the western end of the island. A feature of Crossapol Bay and much of the
sea shore of Coll is the machair. This began as a zone of sand and shells
above the high tide line where no vegetation grew. Some yards further in
from the sea the marram grass began to appear. This is known locally as the
Bents. Its luxuriant root system played a part in preventing the sand from
blowing over and destroying the machair further inland. Cropping or inten-
sive grazing of the fringe zone could have resulted in serious trouble. Fraser
Darling mentioned how marram grass in this fringe zone was cropped in

County Donegal, with the result that a large bridge and some houses were completely enveloped in sand.

Inland from the marram grass the machair supported nitrogen fixing plants and a variety of wild flowers. Fraser Darling, writing in 1947, listed 31 wild flowers that were observed in the Coll machair during the month of July. Since then, I think the number of botanists visiting the island have considerably added to this number. We were not particularly knowledgeable about wild flowers, but during one summer holiday we found buttercup, milkwort, heart's-ease, blood red cranesbill (which we call wild geranium), red clover, wild white clover, bird's-foot trefoil, kidney vetch, wild carrot, lady's bedstraw, daisy, spear thistle, sowthistle, bog pimpernel, forget-me-not, germander speedwell, eyebright, wild thyme, self-heal, frog orchid, Yorkshire fog and woolly fringed moss.

J. A. Steers, writing about the machair in the Western Isles of Scotland said, 'In July the Machair is at its best. On a clear day with a bright sun there are few more beautiful sights than the wide spread of hardy country covered with numerous wild flowers, which give to it not only colour but also scent, and fringed by dazzling white beaches and the blue sea. The surface is broken here and there and exposed the white sand, and in the slight hollows are the lochs, often with many water lilies and the haunt of birds. Inland the natural gives way to the cultivated machair with its crofts and fields, and then comes the peat and the hills. The openness and the vast expanse of sky, sea and hill are unforgettable.'

Well in from the sea where the machair vegetation was luxurious, the soil was rich in lime, and a great variety of snails abounded. From time to time the Laird received letters from people asking him to send them samples of these snails. Doubtless they are of considerable interest, but so far I have had neither the time nor the inclination to study them. The Laird, who worked a 12 hour day on his farm, had understandably some pretty unprintable things to say about people on the mainland who thought he had nothing better to do than go round collecting snails!

On that particular summer day we walked along the high water mark looking for pleasantly shaped pebbles still wet from the receding tide. We had a vague idea that eventually we might be able to polish them in a mechanical tumbler. After about a mile we grew tired of pebble hunting and turned inland across the marram grass. We took a look at a cemetery and two houses behind it. At that time Guy and his wife, Jean, lived in Crossapol House but the other, Caolas, had been deserted for a very long time. It was the most isolated place on Coll. A story was told about an elderly general practitioner of medicine who many years ago retired to this particular house. He was much liked and soon became very popular with everyone on the island. Sometimes fishermen from Tiree dropped anchor in Crossapol Bay and had a drink with him. Eventually he went into decline and had to return to the mainland, where he died. In his last will and testament he made it clear that he wished to be buried in the graveyard close by Crossapol Bay.

Two days after his death the ferry-boat unloaded his crated remains into the motor launch, together with several relations including a wild, one-eyed, bearded brother from Perth. All the able bodied male Collachs paraded at the pier and formed a procession to proceed to the graveyard nine miles away. An ancient van containing the coffin and the principal mourners headed the procession, followed by an even older vehicle laden with whisky bottles, biscuits and cheese. Behind there followed a collection of tractors, each one of which carried at least two people. All went well until the cortege reached the end of the road and had to take to the beach of Crossapol Bay. Very soon the two vans sank down to their axles in the soft wind-blown sand. The men on the tractors tried to pull them out but the towropes snapped. There was nothing else to do but to proceed on foot and carry the old doctor's remains to his last resting place. It was hot and heavy work. Every few minutes the bearers changed and refreshed themselves with biscuits and cheese, washed down with whisky. By the time they reached the burial ground it was nearly dark. An advance party had already dug the grave, assisted by a boatload of men from Tiree.

With solemn reverence the coffin was offered up to the newly dug grave, which proved, however to be a few inches too short. With meticulous care slithers of soil were removed with peat spades until at last a perfect fit was obtained. The Minister read the last rites and returned to the village on the back of one of the tractors. Exhausted by the journey and the digging, the men finished off the whisky salvaged from the van and got to work on the bottles that the Tiree men had brought with them. Perhaps the abundance of spirits and the emotion caused by the bereavement proved to be too much for the wild one eyed brother, for it is related that at this point in the proceedings he climbed up on top of a wall and there, in the moonlight, pointed out to sea and shouted, 'To hell with Tiree', and collapsed. This extraordinary pronouncement was of course the signal for a monumental fight. Early the following morning the womenfolk found their battered husbands in various stages of inebriation along the high water mark of the shores of Crossapol Bay. This was the story as we were told it; it may perhaps contain a grain of truth!

As we walked back from the graveyard we saw no living thing except the birds and seals in the Bay. There were no vehicles on the road as we drove to the village that evening. For no very good reason we had assumed that Guy would take us back to Tobermory the following day, but we discovered that he was over in Tiree and would be back too late to help us. As we went up to the Hotel to discuss the situation I noticed a very smart fishing boat moored up alongside the pier. In the bar were four men playing darts. Alastair, the landlord, told us that they were the crew of the fishing boat and introduced me to their skipper, Alec. He told me that they were heading to Oban the following morning and that he would be glad to give us a lift.

The 'Green Pastures' was only a few months old and built for inshore fishing. In addition to her regular crew, she also had Dougal from the Ministry of Agriculture and Fisheries. He explained that they were carrying out a survey on the distribution of prawns in the area. They planned to take four or five hauls from around the Treshnish, Staffa and Iona, to count the prawns, and to pickle some of them for laboratory examination.

We sailed at 7 am. Doreen and I kept well forward to be out of everyone's way. We passed about a dozen basking sharks before the net was shot. We had never seen this done before and it was fascinating to watch the quietly meticulous way the crew worked as a perfect team. Alec remained in the wheelhouse. One man was stationed on the winch, one in the stern, and one on each quarter. When each haul was brought up the immense bulging net of fish was released on to a large rubber sheet laid out on the deck. There were many cod, some herring and prawns. All the conger eels were instantly despatched. The squids were placed in a separate box. We had never seen monkfish, of which there were quite a few. I think they must really be the most incredibly ugly things in the ocean; they seem to consist of little else but a gigantic mouth which it keeps open all the time. Smaller things innocently swim into this great orifice and find themselves promptly inside the creature's alimentary tract.

Lunchtime soon came round. The taste of cod caught only an hour previously served with mustard sauce is a treat, which most people have probably never experienced. It is hardly necessary to say that we were enormously grateful to Alec and his crew for taking us to the mainland. We were delighted to find that they were obviously very pleased to have us with them and that Doreen should have been the first woman to sail on the Green Pastures. I remember very well how I blushed during lunch when I recalled to myself how I imagined that fishermen were a hard drinking, hard swearing, bunch of men. We very soon discovered that Alec and his crew had all the fine attributes that one looks for but does not often find in a human being. They were devoted to their work, knowledgeable of many things, quietly spoken, full of good humour, deeply religious in a basic sort of way, without any claptrap or nonsense, and physically very fit.

I recalled how once I went sailing for a weekend with a person for whom I had high regard, but once out at sea he went almost berserk with bad language. This, I suppose, was a reaction to his rather dreary daily work and an indication of his lack of confidence in handling his boat. They laughed when I told them I had never been to a football match and how, at school, the only sport that I remotely enjoyed was rowing, because you had to sit down to do it!

During the afternoon we approached Staffa and Alec managed to put the bows of his ship almost into Fingal's Cave. They had never been in so close before and would certainly not have done so on this occasion if we had not been on board. As we headed for the Iona Sound the skipper called me into the wheelhouse, which had some resemblance to the flight deck of an aircraft. The depth of the seabed under the hull was constantly recorded and the tracing made by a shoal of fish could instantly be recognised. The latest thing in ship-to-shore radios literally put the ship on the telephone. If there was a compass I did not see it. Alec relied largely on his Decca navigation aid, which was an incredible box of tricks. As we passed the Abbey on Iona,

Alec demonstrated how it exactly placed the boat's position on the chart. He reckoned it was accurate to within three or four feet.

Between the Ross of Mull and Colonsay the wind blew up and fishing stopped. Michael, Alec's younger brother, took over the wheel and we went down to the cabin. Only by jamming oneself between the bulkhead and the table could one remain sitting upright. For us this was a novel experience but Alec seemed quite unaware of the ship's gyrations. He explained that they fished five days of the week and often had only a few hours' sleep at a time. They fished within about 12 miles of the coast. Sometimes their catch was so poor that it hardly paid the bill for fuel and broken tackle. At other times they would come back on a Saturday with a full hold, and at Leith their wives could look forward to an evening out. He complained of the inadequacy or absence of refrigeration facilities in some of the docks and that sometimes excellent fish were landed but they eventually became fit for nothing but fertiliser. He also complained that British fishermen had to compete with heavily subsidised foreign fleets. Fishing, he told us, was a most dangerous industry and that the accident and mortality rates were relatively high. Last year a friend of his was washed overboard from another boat and was never seen again. He was inclined to agree with me that one day fish breeding by scientists would replace fish hunting.

Green Pastures docked at Oban at 9 pm. The crew would not hear of us going to an hotel. Since they were returning to Leith, they insisted that we spent the night on board. Alec's parting remark was, 'We've left something on ice for you in the hold.' It was about 10 pounds of scampi. This was the end of the seamen's strike and a splendid holiday.

7

Visitors

The slated roofs of many houses in the more exposed places in the Highlands and Islands have proved a problem to their owners. For a long time all may be well but eventually a single slate becomes dislodged. It then requires only a powerful wind to blow through to lift off a whole batch. If at the time the house is isolated and unoccupied, incalculable damage may result. Many have found the answer by making an entirely new roof with corrugated asbestos. Properly done, a secure fireproof structure results. However the work is expensive and the finished job does not look very good until it is mellowed with lichens.

We had already found that a dormer window nicely filled a bad hole and always produced a surplus of slates for mending the smaller holes. At first re-slating seemed easy enough, but we soon discovered that this was a highly skilled trade, which we never mastered. The boys quickly became expert at drilling holes in the slates for the retaining nails and cutting them to the correct shape with a tungsten carbide tipped tile cutter was no problem. The difficulty was in getting the new slates to lie perfectly flat. Quite a small gap would allow the wind to get underneath and, in time, to strip them off. I remembered seeing delightful cottages in Tintagel, Cornwall where the old slated roofs had been covered with several layers of tar. This was obviously effective and the appearance was quite attractive. It seemed, however, that this introduced a fire hazard and I did not fancy the idea of boiling up barrels of tar in the high winds of Coll. I thought that bitumen paint would act as a good seal, but after the first winter it had largely been washed away with several slates blown off.

Some people are suckers for the illustrated brochures produced by manufacturers and I am one of them. I was thrilled to bits on discovering an article explaining how one could repair a disintegrating slate roof by a membrane method. Beautifully illustrated with diagrams the whole business seemed very simple. All you had to do was remove the lichens and other foreign bodies, paint a strip of roof with a solution, and the press into this treated area a length of hessian impregnated with creosote. Finally one applied another coat of waterproofing material. I ordered several hundred feet of the membrane and a few gallons of the appropriate solutions, to be sent to me care of Alastair at the Hotel. I could hardly wait until the next holiday when I could begin the membrane treatment.

In due course I started work. I had, however, chosen a bad day because it was blowing up to force six or seven. I put on thick rubber gloves and applied the first strip of tar-like solution without much difficulty. However, when I began to press in the hessian material I ran into big trouble. The rubber gloves tore into shreds and the sticky membrane wrapped itself around me and everything else except the prepared strip of roof. It was evident that I was being too ambitious. When I cut the 12-foot strip of membrane to half its length I managed to get the stuff to stick down firmly and applied the second coat. By the time I had the membrane firmly fixed onto a dormer roof I felt, and probably looked, like a fly in the middle of giant flypaper. Once during my earlier efforts I panicked when I found that both my feet were firmly stuck to the roof. When I eventually freed myself, getting down the ladder proved no easy task since both my hands and feet were inclined to adhere to the rungs. The only way to clean myself up was to wash in paraffin. I could not possibly go indoors without changing my clothes and shoes.

When I finished the roof at Port na Luing I thought I had an absolutely first class watertight structure with every single slate securely covered and sealed. However, waterproofing the roof was only half the battle because rain rarely came down vertically on Coll. It usually hurtled at the house more or less horizontally and quickly penetrated through the eaves, entered cracks in the masonry, and saturated the walls. We sealed the eaves with broad strips of waterproof tape. Instead of attempting to repoint the outside walls, the entire surface was painted with two coats of black bitumen based paint. It was quite impossible to fix guttering with conventional brackets. Instead we hammered lengths of planking under the eaves using six-inch nails, driving them into cracks between the granite blocks whenever we could find them. The planks were painted with bitumen and covered with membrane. Then the guttering was attached with galvanised nails through holes drilled every 12 inches along the inside edge.

The reader may wonder what connection there can be between this description of the membrane treatment and the chapter heading 'Visitors'; I will explain. For four successive holidays I spent most of my time on the roof slapping on the membrane. From this vantage point I was able to see anyone approaching the house by land, sea, or air. Depending on the time of day I had time to call out to Doreen or one of the children to put the kettle on for coffee or tea, or to fetch out the glasses for more serious refreshment.

I could hear the noise of Jimmy's tractor some time before it appeared from behind the hill. It was always a pleasure to see him with Margaret perched on the back making their way slowly towards us. Long before we ever found Coll the starter motor had gone wrong, so Jimmy parked his machine on the brow of a hill beside his house and started it by releasing the brake and letting out the clutch when it was going fast enough. At Port na Luing he always left the engine running. It had no lights; sometimes on a dark night we wondered how they managed to get home.

We soon fell into a sort of fixed routine. Margaret, Doreen and the children would go into the house and have a gossip while Jimmy and I would go off for a stroll. Often enough he was tired out after his day on the farm, but if there was ever any unfinished work he would be the first to give me a hand. It was he who dug out a drainage trench around the house. He replaced the slates after a gale before we had finished treating the roof. On that occasion both he and Margaret spent the night in the house, which finally put an end to the ridiculous notion that the place was haunted. However their dog spent the night with them, just in case!

The heaviest job that Jimmy and I ever did together was to move the Jøtul stove from the back of the Land Rover into the corner of the drawing room. We had in the previous months given a great deal of thought to the question of heating. We needed a fire which would burn peat, driftwood and rubbish, which would stay in all night, warm a large section of the house, heat water for cooking and look attractive. The Scandinavian Jøtul did all these things but was a colossal weight. Apparently it had been quite a headache transferring it from the ferry-boat into the launch. I found it in a crate behind the Hotel. With help from a number of men working on the new pier we loaded it into the Land Rover without much trouble. However, down at Port na Luing the situation seemed hopeless until Jimmy arrived. By means of some pit props that had been washed up in Crossapol Bay we slowly rolled the crate into the drawing room, and finally stood it up in the corner. The job took nearly an hour. Doreen, seeing our state of exhaustion, produced an emergency bottle of whisky. I am ashamed to say that between us we drank the lot and fell asleep.

Next morning, in spite of a terrible head, I ran a length of angle iron from the concrete floor behind the stove, through an aperture in the bedroom floor and through a corresponding hole in the roof. The boys and I bolted four-foot lengths of asbestos pipe to the angle iron, sealed them together with fire clay and joined the lower end of this chimney to the back of the stove by means of an enormous U bend affair, which was also made of asbestos. It only remained for us to close the gap in the roof with some flashing and to put on a cowl. It looked rather good. The green stove, looking like a mighty Dalek, seemed hungry for fuel and anxious to show us what it could do. We filled it up with shavings and driftwood and very soon had a roaring fire. The chimney pipe radiated a tremendous amount of heat, the drawing room and bedroom above became uncomfortably hot, and a couple of kettles rapidly came to the boil. Quite suddenly our rejoicing gave way to utter despair; the wind veered to the north and the stove was no longer our slave but our master. It began spitting out great jets of thick black smoke. Closing the flue simply made matters worse, and opening all the windows did not seem to improve the situation. I think that it must have been the ignition of some tar on a piece of driftwood that produced such smog so that there was no alternative but to evacuate Port na Luing.

Coughing, spluttering and with eyes running, all six of us drove over to Margaret for help and consolation. It came as a bit of an anticlimax when, having told her our tale of woe, she exclaimed that everyone's stove smoked terribly in Coll when the wind was in the north. Later we put on an extra four feet of chimney and a patent 'smokeless' cowl. Now the smoke produced by a northerly wind is just, but only just, tolerable. Fortunately for us, the wind normally blew from the south-west.

While the house was filling up with smoke we noticed an interesting thing. Not all the smoke was blowing out of the windows; some was finding its way out through the stonework at one end of the drawing room. We removed the remains of the plaster over this area and discovered that this was the site of an old doorway, which had been filled in with rubble. It proved to be quite a simple matter to remove the rubble and fit in a window. It happened to be a pretty wet day when Doreen and I were doing this. The children filled in the cracks between the granite with Polyfilla and then applied two coats of white emulsion paint.

Back home in Hampshire, a neighbour helped me to build a staircase out of parana pine. We brought it up in bits on the roof rack of the car. By the time it was assembled and fixed into position the drawing room really became worthy of its name.

Across the two vertical beams supporting the bedroom floor, the roof above and the staircase to one side, we fixed a bookshelf and, at a lower level, a desk. We had previously obtained a formidable looking lectern at an auction sale in Fordingbridge. This was fitted on to the desk and is now called the Scriptorium. It served as a useful depository for writing things, bills and building material brochures. The lectern itself is quite a weight and is useful for pressing flowers.

We badly needed somewhere to dry our clothes and air the bedding. We were getting tired of the clothesline slung between the flooring joists in the drawing room. The Jøtul stove stood in one corner three feet away from the wall. In this area around the asbestos chimney pipe we constructed a triangular shaped airing cupboard with slatted shelves. We soon discovered that the chimney became so hot that the clothes next to it were scorched. It was not until the asbestos pipe had been encased with a collar of wire netting that the cupboard was safe to use. A second smaller cupboard was built around the chimney as it ran in the corresponding corner of the bedroom above.

I discovered that it was possible to paint pictures on glazed tiles with watercolours. There was no need to use egg tempera or other media provided that the brush was kept fairly dry. The outline of the picture was first made in Indian ink. When finished, a spray of clear polyurethane varnish protected the painting. A dozen tiles depicting Scottish castles were stuck and grouted together on the back of the mantelpiece supporting the airing cupboard. Other tiles showing salmon flies, pictures from Edward Lear's Nonsense Rhymes and windmills were stuck on one of the bathroom walls later on. Besides giving an air of hygiene to the smallest room in the house, they also served as something to look at when meditating on the loo.

In time all manner of folk who came to Coll heard about our house and came down to see us. Quite a few became lost on the way and gave up the search. By the very nature of the island, holidaymakers in Coll were always the sort of people who wanted to escape for a while from the lunatic life on the mainland. For the most part they were keen amateur bird watchers, botanists or geologists. We were always glad to see them and sometimes they would stay all day helping us with the building. To help them find their way around the island more easily we mounted a six-inch to the mile map of the island on one end of the drawing room. On this map we stuck labelled paper flags of interesting things we saw or found.

The botanists who came to Coll were, I am sure, delightful people if you got to know them, but they always struck me as a bit austere. The ladies always seemed to wear heavy tweeds and, of course, described their finds in a Latin jargon incomprehensible to me. By contrast, the geologists seemed to like their pint of beer, and, as you might expect, were big jolly men armed with crowbars and pickaxes. For all I knew they might have had a stick of dynamite and a length of fuse hidden away in their hip pockets. The ornithologists had bird-like features and were inclined to hop about. They constantly wore a pair of field glasses round their necks; I really believe that some of them went to bed with them on. They would suddenly jump up in the middle of a meal and announce that they had just heard the call of a particular bird, which was inaudible to everyone else. They were sensitive and gentle folk, whom I liked very much.

The largest number of visitors we entertained at one time in Port na Luing was 34. It was a pleasant afternoon. Doreen was working in the end bedroom and I was painting the inside of one of the upstairs windows. I glanced out and saw the children coming back in the boat. One of them was waving and pointing to the track that led down to the house. There to my dismay I saw three separate groups of people heading towards us led by a Land Rover and flanked by Fenella and Fiona on ponies from Acha. I suddenly remembered that I had asked Mairi and Ronnie with their children from Crossapol House to tea and supposed it was just coincidence that about half the other children on the island and their parents were all visiting us at the same time.

My instinctive reaction was to hide under the bed. However Doreen walked on to the patio as cool as a cucumber and welcomed everyone as if she had been waiting for them all afternoon. There was just enough food because Margaret had given us a tin of scones and the girls had made cakes that were still warm. There weren't enough cups so everyone had to take it in turns for a cup of tea or a fizzy drink. For a while there was utter pandemonium while the children explored the house, climbed up the ladders and generally amused themselves. It was late by the time the last child had departed with it's Mum and Dad. We were exhausted but pleased that we had been able to entertain such a multitude in a house which two years before had been a derelict ruin. Port na Luing was most certainly very much alive again!

Sunday was very much a rest day in the Hebrides. Only essential work, such as milking, was undertaken on the Sabbath. One soon lost track of time and after a little while one was inclined to have a rather vague notion of the day of the week. With so much work to be crammed into a fortnight's holiday we often worked flat out every day. On one Sunday I was busy making a hole in the wall to fix in an extra window in the kitchen. I had already spent several days on the job but appeared to have met my Waterloo. A gigantic granite block had got stuck in the orifice and no amount of chipping away with the cold chisel would free it. Sweating and saying rather profane things

about Scottish granite, I suddenly realised that I was not alone. Standing behind me was an unexpected visitor – the Minister! Instead of administering
a reprimand, he removed his coat, stuck a crowbar under the block, levered
it upwards enabling me to pull it free. In fact he didn't put his jacket on for
another couple of hours and helped me to get the window frame into position.
He stayed for supper. Such was our celebration that night on the occasion of
completing the window that I had to drive the Land Rover pretty slowly
over to the Manse and back.

It is evident that we never lost the chance of obtaining voluntary labour
whenever the opportunity presented itself. I think our visitors who found
themselves put to work must have enjoyed it or they would not have come
back for more punishment. John fell into our trap most beautifully. I spotted
him from the roof; he was walking down the hillside carrying a rucksack
and suitcase. He asked if we would sell him some milk. Cunningly we asked
him in for a meal. He explained that he was hitchhiking on £50 to the
Argentine but had been side tracked to Mull and inexplicably carried on to
Coll. He had walked the eight miles from the village looking for somewhere
to camp and certainly looked pretty exhausted. We put him up for a week,
during which time he did a tremendous amount of work mixing concrete
and laying the foundations for the patio in front of the house. He lost his
way again after he left us and never made it to the Argentine. He ended up
in France, where, we were told, he joined the Foreign Legion.

Another of our innocent victims who did his bit in the rebuilding of Port
na Luing was the War Graves Inspector. We found him in the back bar of
the hotel enjoying a pint. He told us that he was trying to get a lift out to the
graveyard at Crossapol. We were more than delighted to take him because
there was an old bath, which we were anxious to move down to the house,
lying at Breachacha Farm. Doreen and I had been unable to lift it when we
tried on our way down to the village and all the men on the farm had been
out. The poor chap was obviously not used to such strenuous exercise, but
the three of us managed to get it into the back of the Land Rover and deliver
it to our front door. We gave him lunch and more beer, sending him on his
way rejoicing.

The boys of Cheltenham College referred to their institution as 'Coll'.
John, Christopher, and Heddon discovered the island on the map and decided to go there one summer holiday in order to write up their experience
for a school prize. Quite by chance we were given their names. Of course,
we lost no time in sending them information and a detailed map of the west
end of the island, pointing out that by far and away the best place to camp
was within a stone's throw of Port na Luing. Their holiday started before
ours, but when we arrived it began raining and they were glad to vacate
their tent to stay with us. At the time I was putting in a ceiling in our bedroom and they did a splendid job painting the beams black and putting
white paint on the fibreboard ceiling. It cleared up next day so we all had a
marvellous time excavating a spring on the hillside behind the house. We
carried up tons of rock from the old pier, mixed cement and concrete, and

made a 2000 gallon dam, which we connected to the house by means of an alkathene pipe. By the time we had finished all this we were all utterly exhausted. When the boys left us they said that they had never before had such a wonderful time and that they would be back next year!

One of our most welcome guests was Indie. I had ordered a 1000 gallon galvanised tank to collect the rainwater but the first tank was badly bashed on the cargo boat from Glasgow. Months later the second arrived and I found it anchored down by Calum behind the petrol pump. It looked a monster and the track down to Port na Luing was a quagmire. I knew Indie had a tractor and large trailer and he cheerfully agreed to bring my tank down. A few days later he arrived at dusk and we all saw one of the finest examples of tractor driving anyone can hope to see. Without a hitch he reversed the trailer round two right angle bends deep in mud and tipped the tank onto the concrete base as easily as if he was unloading a sack of potatoes.

We were delighted one day to drive Mary down to our house for tea. The last time she had been there had been about 40 years previously. At first she hardly recognised the place, but after a while she recalled some of her previous visits. In the old days the kitchen served as the sitting room and bedroom too. Our drawing room, with its concrete floor, functioned as a cattle byre before the doorway, which we had discovered, had been filled up with rubble. Fishing nets and cattle fodder were stored in the attic upstairs, which we had converted into bedrooms. Mrs MacLean, the mistress of the household, would row round to Arinagour for the Port na Luing messages. If it was too rough to go by boat, she walked and knitted a sock on the way to the village and it's fellow on her return! Sometimes folk from Tiree would row over for an evening's Ceilidh and return in the early hours by the way that they had come. They were certainly a tough lot in those days! Mary gave us the Minister's lectern which she had removed from the abandoned Free Church Chapel. An enormous recess carved out of the surface to lodge a turnip watch, tells a story!

Angus had been fishing for lobsters since the day he had learnt to walk. From the top of the roof I could see the tattered red sail of his boat out at sea. My cry, 'Angus is coming', produced wild activity. The children at once grabbed their gumboots and anoraks and ran up the hill behind the house to fly a kite or hoist a coloured polythene bag on to a pole and announce their presence. By the time his boat entered our bay they would be ready to haul it in and make fast the anchor in the sand. He looked a bit like Father Christmas, and the children loved him. Often he came up to the house for a dram and then took the children out in his boat to pull up the lobster pots. He could be away for hours. He had a very sound knowledge of seamanship and I trusted him implicitly with the care of my family out at sea.

At that time it no longer paid to send lobsters to Glasgow. The entire catch was stowed in floating boxes and sent to Oban or Billingsgate. Then (the late 1960s) winter prices reached about a pound sterling for every pound of lobster, but the bad weather often resulted in a small catch. The work was hard and often hazardous. What was really required was a tidal pond, protected from gales, in which the surplus of the summer catch could have been stored until the winter. However the cost was prohibitive. Angus always left one of his creels for the children in the channel between the house and Soa. Every day when the weather was fair the four of them rowed out, emptied and rebaited the creel. Usually they came back with at least one lobster and several crabs. When they went out with Angus they always returned with a lobster or two and a bucket full of crabs.

We had never before cared much about eating lobsters, finding them to be rather indigestible. However after a few days we found ourselves with four or five so it seemed worthwhile to try to master the art of cooking them. I had been given a book on the art of French cooking, which consisted of 863 pages of gastronomic delight, profusely illustrated with coloured photographs, each of which produced a reflex flow of saliva and anticipatory rumbling of the intestines. I rejected at once the preparation of Lobster Americaine and Lobster Bordelaise since each one of these methods required that one should cut up the creature while still alive. I found it difficult enough to kill the unfortunate animal by plunging in into boiling water. The method we eventually adopted was to boil the lobsters well, remove the flesh, cover it with hot tomato sauce, and serve immediately with slices of hard-boiled eggs. The tomato sauce was made by cutting up 6 lbs of tomatoes into small pieces and putting them into a stew pan with 5 tablespoonfuls of olive oil, a pinch of salt and pepper, and a chopped clove of garlic. The pan was covered and the contents cooked on a low stove for half an hour. The sauce was strained through a fine sieve, a knob of butter was added, and it was heated up again. It was poured over the hot lobster and served on a very hot plate. It was delicious, but the meat of one large lobster was required per person, which was a bit expensive if you lived on the mainland!

Inspired by Angus, we bought a 12 feet long fibreglass rowing boat. It was shipped from Glasgow and spent several days on the pier in the village. Some said it looked fine and had nice lines, but would not be any good and would hole if it touched a rock. It should have been made of wood! In fact it has served us well for nearly 40 years and requires very little maintenance! Polystyrene blocks under each thwart give good buoyancy. On either side of the keel are grab handles which one can hold on to if she capsizes – we have never had to use them. Perhaps we have been over cautious but we have always carried self-igniting flares and worn life jackets.

As soon as we got the boat down to Port na Luing, we went out fishing. In the summer mackerel can come in by the thousand. We caught them with a line attached to six hooks dressed with feathers, with a lead weight on the end, called a darrow. Once I thought I had an exceptionally large fish . . . the more I pulled, the stronger the returning pulls. It was quite a while before I realised that my line was tangled up with Doreen's under the boat, and we were trying to pull each other overboard!

One evening, rowing back into our harbour, I heard a squeaking noise. I thought it was coming from the rowlocks, but it wasn't. We saw two baby otters having fun sliding down a little sand bank, just above the high water mark. As we pulled the boat in, Doreen commented, 'I don't suppose many people have ever seen such a delightful sight.'

Sometimes, one can catch a fish on each hook at the same time and can land too many. We swapped them for vegetables. It's a great thrill to catch a fish on a home-made hook. You take a suitable bit of wire, bend it, sharpen the end and fashion the barb with a fine file.

One summer after months of drought, mushrooms sprung up everywhere overnight. Not the small button things you buy in a tin, but huge succulent specimens. Some were as large as saucers. They were in the fields by their thousands for days and days. We ate masses of them but have since wished we had thought of trying to dry them or preserve them in some way.

In the June holiday of 1967 we ate clams (scallops) with practically every meal. It came about in this way. During the spring of that year Dr David Bellamy, marine biologist, gave a talk on the wireless. He maintained that salt water pollution was killing off seaweeds and that in some cases productivity of the seaweed beds had been reduced by as much as 90 per cent. He said that the beds in the unpolluted waters of Saint Abbs were nine times more productive than similar ones in the polluted waters of the Durham coast. He appealed to members of the British Sub-Aqua Club to collect and weigh the stalks of the seaweed *Laminariea hyperboria* in various coastal waters. This scheme, called Operation Kelp, was fairly widely publicised and written up in the skin-divers' journal *Triton*.

I wrote to Dr Bellamy, telling him that we would be glad to put up some of his skin-diving marine biologists. Of course, I also had the slightly ulterior motive of hoping that when they were not actually skin-diving, they would be able to help me with the rebuilding. Dr Bellamy telephoned and said that he would be glad if we could look after two men from Durham and a friend. Doreen and I realised that we were taking a slight gamble, but we were not disappointed.

We met David, a graduate of Durham University, Dai, a student and son of a Welsh miner, and Colin, a skin-diving freelance journalist, on the pier. They were a tough, jovial set of men, whose hair, Doreen pointed out, was a good deal shorter than mine. Apart from their personal luggage, they had six cylinders for compressed air, a petrol driven compressor, wet suits, lead belts, an echo sounder, underwater cameras and laboratory equipment.

Everyone very soon knew that the three skin-divers were staying with us. For the first few days they were in great demand for locating and repairing anchorages. At last they were able to settle down to algae research and, as I suspected, they reported very dense sublitoral seaweed beds only a few yards from the low water mark in our bay and around Soa. They also found a few specimens which were a feature of Mediterranean waters and had not been seen on British shores before. They always took several pillowcases with them in the underwater forages, which they filled with seaweeds and sometimes with lobsters and clams. On occasion they came back with about 50 clams for us to feast on. In addition to supplying us with seafood, they helped put in the fourth dormer window and lay the wooden floors in the kitchen, hall and bathroom. We bade them farewell a few days before the end of our holiday. They left behind them a large bottle of formaldehyde, which I liberally applied to some green slime on the kitchen walls. It worked most effectively but after a few minutes the fumes were so powerful that we were again driven out of our house with streaming eyes and choking throats.

In 1971 my old friend Michael Gilkes sailed round a number of Hebridean islands, inspecting anchorages and noting the harbour facilities that had been described by the Clyde Cruising Club. He got as far as St Kilda but it was too rough to land. One of the crew of his yacht the 'Foggy Dew' was Adlard Coles, a much-respected author and publisher of yachting journals. Later Adlard published Mike's log under the delightful title *Taking Coles to the Coirebhreacain*. On 6th June Mike dropped anchor in our bay and I rowed out to collect the crew. Bill Dunn, George Orwell's brother-in-law, passed me his tin leg and clambered on board followed by Adlard, Lorimer, and a retired brigadier named David Wilson. Mike of course left his yacht last of all. David played a pleasant tune on his accordion as I rowed them to Port na Luing. Mike wrote in his log, 'Our friends, who have made a splendid job of restoring the ruined house here, received us royally. Neighbours arrived on tractors and Land Rovers from all around and a splendid evening resulted. Despite pressure to stay ashore, a reasonably coherent crew returned to ship about midnight.'

Neillie John was one of the great characters of Coll and there are many stories about him. Once, it is said, Robert Sturgeon took him out in a boat lifting lobster pots. They were accompanied by a large, cheerful, heavily tweeded lady, who kept saying 'super'. (You must know the sort of person!) They sailed quite a way towards the east end of the island. When they turned back Neillie got under a tarpaulin and refreshed himself with whisky. After a time he indicated to Robert that he wanted to land and relieve himself. Once ashore, Robert told the tweeded lady to follow Neillie closely and he would show her the sights. Neillie eventually arrived back in much discomfort and embarrassment about to burst!

Sometimes, at the hotel Neillie would drink too much and stagger about upsetting the guests. Alastair would throw him out to sober up. On one such occasion he thought he might find a drink or two at Port na Luing. We saw an apparently empty car coming down the hillside with all its doors flapping like wings. We found Neillie crouched under the steering wheel. I happened to be outside the house when the greatly refreshed Neillie staggered out. 'There's an old woman in there' he said, 'she gave me plenty of drams and wouldn't let me pay for them.' The old woman was my mother! He returned up the hill with the broken doors still flapping!

Once, Dr Van de Vries, a Dutch man, who lived in the Lodge and flew to and from the island by helicopter, announced, 'Today you must have mine helicopter'. I wasn't too keen on the idea because I had been in a chopper crash in the Navy. The pilot had been a stupid idiot who started larking about after take off. One of the rotor blades hit the ground and the machine broke up. I had woken up in the sick bay, where an Irish Surgeon Captain RN had said to me, 'What's it feel like to be alive?' It was remarkable that no one was killed and I was fortunate to escape with just a cut on my hand, but my fear of helicopters had continued. However, on this occasion, it was a beautiful still day, the sea was shimmering and I was determined not to let the opportunity slip away. Captain Salt landed on our beach and took four passengers at a time to Staffa and Fingal's Cave. It was the most thrilling experience and I completely lost my fear of choppers! Pity that helicopters had not been invented in Felix Mendelssohn's time . . . how he would have loved that trip! When Dr De Vries left he said 'You too should have ein helicopter!'

8

Flotsam and Jetsam and Things

One of the advantages of being so close to the sea is that we have been able to pick up a whole variety of flotsam and jetsam. In the early years we found many of the original green glass fishing floats in their rope nets. Later these were replaced by aluminium and then plastic floats which, although they may have been much more effective, are not so attractive hanging in the house! Driftwood of every shape and size including fish boxes (now alas, also made in plastic) was utilised throughout Port na Luing.

On one occasion Doreen decided that we really needed a dustpan. Stephen, then aged seven knew exactly what to do. He disappeared along the coast for about an hour and returned, triumphant, with a splendid red dustpan. With its barnacles removed it served us well for a long time! From then on, whenever we needed anything, Stephen was sent out to scour the coast. His finds included a wonderful ship's lantern, a wooden elephant, distress flares, extinct land mines and a collection of Dutch clogs! A 'Bus stop' sign is mounted on a post outside the gate. It was rather a shame that an ancient double-decker bus, which was touring the island for several days, causing chaos on the single track road, couldn't possibly get down to us and park by the sign!

Sadly, many of our finds must have been the result of disasters at sea. From our vantage point at Port na Luing we have witnessed a few.

A number of ships have been wrecked on Coll's shores. The Dominion liner 'Nessmore' went aground in 1895 with 600 cattle on board, but thanks to the help of the islanders most of the animals were safely brought ashore. In the sands of Gorton Bay you can still see the remains of the Norwegian barque 'Harmony', from which one of the crew was drowned while swimming to the headland. Quite recently a Finnish vessel was wrecked on a lee shore but re-floated after a few days. An official of Lloyds and a customs officer were quickly on the scene. By all accounts the latter was a portly gentleman and unable to climb aboard by means of a rope ladder. He spent his stay on the island in the hotel bar, during which time some of the ship's liquor 'fell overboard'. It is said that his report must have been the shortest ever submitted by an officer of the Customs and Excise; he simply wrote 'wreck inaccessible'.

Towards the end of our first summer holiday at Port na Luing the tail end of Hurricane Faith hit Coll and we very nearly had a wreck on our doorstep. At the time Roy and Bunny were with us again, and also David's friend Richard. He had never been away from home before and we were a bit concerned lest he might become homesick. We need not have worried because he entered into the spirit of things at once. He was soon doing as much work as anyone. Indeed he enjoyed himself so much that he persuaded his parents and two brothers to come up with him again the following year. At that time we had done nothing to the roof over the kitchen end of the house and we could see stars through the holes. Whenever it rained it leaked like a riddle. The windows were as yet unglazed and there was no floor in the kitchen. It was a simple matter to pitch a tent on the mud to make an excellent dormitory for the three boys. With the third dormer window installed Roy and Bunny had quite a good bedroom and the girls slept in the corridor.

We saw high stratocumulus clouds while we were surfing at Bally Haugh Bay and in the evening we heard a storm warning for our area on the shipping forecast. We moved the Land Rover to the sheltered side of the house, brought in the empty alkathene tanks and everything else which had been left outside. Soon the wind coming through the eaves was causing an unpleasant draught making a noise like organ pipes and causing the paraffin lamps to burn erratically. However we were a bit more comfortable after we had stuffed bits of fibreglass into the gaps. We went to bed expecting big things to happen and were a bit disappointed when the wind suddenly dropped. We imagined that the hurricane had gone off like a damp squib.

Early next morning it blew up to gale force. The ferry-boat gave Coll a wide berth. It began to rain and torrents of sea spray splashed over the house. Some water got under the door and produced a small flood in the hall. There were several leaks in the roof over the drawing room end, which we had to collect in buckets and empty baked bean tins. It was Bunny who noticed a small yacht anchored at the entrance to our harbour. We recognised it as Guy's boat with passengers from Tiree. Roy and I reckoned that if we stood on either side of the harbour entrance we would each be able to throw a line to the yacht to make her secure and get the passengers ashore. We yelled to Guy to come in but either he did not hear us or thought little of our plan because he soon weighed anchor and headed out past Soa.

We watched his progress through binoculars from one of the bedroom windows. It was a sickening sight. Every few moments the small boat disappeared in the troughs between the great waves and eventually she disappeared altogether near a rock. We were all convinced that she had gone down. While we wondered what we could do Neillie Angus arrived on a tractor. He told us that Jimmy, Willie the shepherd, and others at Breachacha Farm had also seen the boat disappear. They thought there was a chance that she was aground on the lee shore but to take anyone off they would need all the help they could muster.

While Neillie Angus drove back up the hill, Roy, the children and I put on our foul-weather clothes. We collected some ropes and followed the tractor in the Land Rover as far as Breachacha Farm. From there we had to walk, as there was no track through the heather. It was hard going but Stephen kept up with the rest of us pretty well. At last we came upon a small sheltered bay near the headland where, by incredible luck and good seamanship, Guy

The Port na Luing bus stop.

had been able to drop anchor. He was too far out for us to hail him but the boat seemed to be intact.

Jimmy, Willy and Neillie Angus took it in turns to stand watch over the yacht throughout the night while we, in the comparative comfort of Port na Luing, watched the drama out at sea. An hour or so before we had discovered the yacht safely in the bay, Willie had telephoned Alastair, who had in turn telephoned the lifeboat at Mallaig. Later we discovered that the lifeboat set out twice. On the first occasion she was called back by wireless since it was thought that she had answered a false alarm. However the second call could not be cancelled because by the time we all got back to Breachacha Farm we found that the telephone lines had been blown down. As there was no wireless station on Coll, and mobile 'phones had not yet been invented, there was no means of turning the lifeboat back.

Shortly after midnight a searchlight shone on Port na Luing. A few moments later the whole of Breachacha Bay was lit up by parachute flares. We saw the lights of the lifeboat. The swaying and dipping lights were indication enough of the devil of a time those men were experiencing. The boat circled several times and did not leave until first light. We watched in darkness because we dared not put on a light lest they might think that we were trying to send a signal. How I wished my knowledge of the Morse code was not just limited to the SOS and 'U', ('You are standing into danger'), and that I could flash a torch to tell them that the yacht was safe so that they could return home to Mallaig.

Next morning Alastair managed to launch a rubber dinghy and take off a man, his wife and their 12-year-old boy. He also took food for Guy.

Nearly three years later John Murray wrote an article about Charles Henderson, who was the coxswain of the Mallaig lifeboat, in the March 1969 edition of *The Scottish Field*. Tommy Ralston, the lifeboat's mechanic, had something to say about the night and his coxswain, 'One night in particular there was a small boat got into trouble on a lee shore on Coll; into a hole among the rocks with the entrance blocked by three half-tide reefs that were being absolutely hammered by the breakers. We lay off for a bit, then Charlie decided to take us straight in by the light of searchlights and parachute flares. There wasn't a hope, of course, and we thought the boat would have to be written off; but having made the attempt, Charlie *reversed* out, calm as you like, and the people were rescued from the shore. I've never seen anything like it, and I was a fisherman for 16 years.'

I wrote to Charlie Henderson and asked him if he could give us some more information about that night. In his letter he said, 'We did spend a pretty miserable night outside Port na Luing on that occasion. We tried several times to get in through the narrow entrance to where the yacht was lying, but with the shallow water at the entrance, between the rollers, we could distinctly hear the shingle rolling, and very near the lifeboat forefoot, so we gave it up until daybreak when we had another look, and came to the conclusion that the vessel was anchored quite safely in the bay, and that the occupants could be taken off quite easily from the shore.' He enclosed a copy of the report he had sent to the Royal National Lifeboat Institution, which I think is worth repeating verbatim:

Lifeboat Station – Mallaig.   Date of Service 5th and 6th September, 1966.

Name of Lifeboat – E. M. M. Gordon Cubbins

The lifeboat was launched to search for a boat reported overdue between Tiree and Coll. After being about an hour under way we were recalled, being told by coastguard Southend that the boat was safe.

Twenty minutes after reaching the station, we were told that the boat was again in difficulties, and launched immediately.

On reaching the boat, several attempts were made to get in to her, but it proved impossible, owing to the ebbing tide and darkness. During one of these attempts a heavy sea broke aboard, shearing the loud hailer and cracking one of the wheelhouse windows slightly.

At daylight it was seen that the narrow entrance to the bay was breaking heavily across, and that the casualty appeared to be lying safely. One more attempt was made to get in, but as we felt that if the occupants could be taken off easily by the Life Saving Apparatus (L.S.A.) who were standing ashore, we did not deem that the risk of loss of, or damage to, the Lifeboat was justified.

After a message to the Hon. Sec. the Lifeboat went to Arinagour, where we told the L.S.A. people that we felt that they should take the occupants ashore. This was done, the skipper remaining on board. The L.S.A. confirmed our opinion that there was no risk to the skipper, so the Lifeboat returned to the station.

(sd) CHARLES HENDERSON
Coxswain-in-Charge.

After a while the storm abated and Guy sailed to Arinagour. We met him and his passengers in the Hotel bar. None seemed the worst for their adventure. Never once, they told us, in all that wind, did Guy's kilt ever blow above his knees!

On a very dark and warm summer evening we suddenly saw what appeared to be the lights of Blackpool approaching our house. I grabbed one of those portable foghorns, which were used by tractor drivers and spelt out 'U' in Morse. A few moments later we heard her dropping anchor a few hundred yards from our front door. David and I went over in the boat and a crewman threw us a rope and rope ladder. There were several distress rockets on the companion way up to the bridge. The captain was a fairly young Irishman dressed only in shorts. He thought he was some eight miles eastwards. He had sent out an SOS but there was so much static he doubted if any station had heard him. I showed him exactly where he was and told him to blow his hooter if he had to abandon ship and I would turn the Land Rover towards him with the lights on.

I made my way back to my boat but there was no sign of David. The ship was beginning to list to port and the crew were getting out a lifeboat. I smelt the agreeable odour of cooking and in the galley I found an enormously fat Irish cook and David tucking into bacon and eggs.

In the early morning light we could see her propeller, but with the high tide the 'MV Blackthorne', en route from Belfast to Glasgow, in ballast, floated off the rocks. Later we heard that she did get to Glasgow but with all pumps running flat out. I told Alec that morning about our adventure. Apparently the Blackthorne's SOS had got through and he and others had spent a pretty miserable night vainly searching for her along the coast at the east end. Sadly, a few years later, we were told the Blackthorne collided with another vessel in the Thames estuary and a man was drowned.

Many people in Coll remembered the wreck of the 'Nevada' in 1942. In a flat calm sea, on a foggy day, the 7000 ton vessel sailed from Glasgow to join a convoy bound for South Africa. She had an African crew and a French skipper, who lost his way, struck the north-east coast of Coll, and stuck his vessel fast between a rock and the coast of the island. So perfectly had she become berthed that the crew were able to step ashore, and the men of Coll got aboard without any trouble at all. At the time it seemed almost as if the whole thing was a preconceived and deliberate act; some Collachs declared that it was 'savatage'.

The cargo consisted of NAAFI supplies. The hatch covers were off in minutes. The less expensive tins of cigarettes were thrown overboard and only the better sort landed. For the first time some of the women took to smoking. It was told how one housewife, fearing that the Customs and Excise officers might discover her, flattened several thousand cigarettes with a clothes iron, stuck them onto the kitchen wall, and then covered the whole lot with flour paste and wallpaper. History did not relate how they subsequently tasted!

Although spirits were not so plentiful as in Compton Mackenzie's *Whisky Galore*, there were enough bottles to satisfy most people's thirst for quite a long time. Two men landed a couple of crates and hid them under an up-turned boat, only to discover the following day that they had been pinched. In the village they angrily exclaimed that if it had not been for the fact that they were dishonest, they would certainly have called the police. Another disappointed man staggered ashore with several gallons of a clear fluid, which he took to be gin, only later to discover that it was surgical spirit. A vast quantity of brown shoes to fit left feet only, South African policemen's uniforms and NAAFI caps were found in the holds. This apparel became the dress of the day for some of the islanders, though they never did find the crate with shoes for right feet! The ship's cat was nearly left stranded. Eventually it was observed and taken ashore in a drawer from the skipper's cabin. A Coll man, with a sack full of cigarettes, was caught by a Customs and Excise officer – he gave his name and address as the Church of Scotland Minister! Perhaps the most valuable loot of all consisted of several suit cases stuffed full of South African bank notes, which a member of the crew managed to get back to the mainland. Many years later he was caught trying to unload his ill-gotten gains in Switzerland.

A contingent of Royal Air Force men on the island rigged a bosun's chair and helped themselves. It was related that the exercise was well worth their while. The RAF were soon followed by the salvage men, who blasted a track through from the road and put up a crane on the rock beside the ship. They were too late as a gale shifted the wreck and she broke in half. Some 20 years later our skin-diving friends went down to take a look. The phosphor bronze propeller was nowhere to be found, but they saw a considerable quantity of copper tubing. They said that the jeeps in the hold still had inflated tyres. Colin managed to buy the salvage rights. A year later he came back with some friends and they were able to take off the copper and some

'Nevada' gun mounted outside the hotel.

other non-ferrous metals, some of which hang on a beam in our drawing room! Even if one day all the cargo is removed, it will still be worth visiting the Nevada, for it is now the home of hundreds of fish and lobsters.

On the stern of the Nevada was mounted a four inch gun. In 1992 the Hyndburn sub-aqua club freed it from the deck. With the help of giant bags, filled with compressed air, they managed to float it to the surface. It was then towed round to the new pier where it was lifted with a crane, and taken to the Hotel garden – a grim memorial of Coll in Hitler's war. (See *Coll Magazine* 1993)

After the war the London cargo vessel 'Tapti', sailing in ballast with a crew of 63, sank in a gale off the Island of Soa, a few hundred yards from Port na Luing. Thanks to the Mallaig lifeboat nobody was drowned but very little was salvaged. One evening the skin divers recharged their air bottles and went down to investigate. They found her lying pretty deeply and in a bad state of disintegration. A shaft of sunlight illuminated the barnacle-encrusted ship's wheel; they described it as one of the loveliest things they had ever seen. They went down again with a crowbar to try to free it but without success. Perhaps it was just as well, for on dry land it would surely have lost much of its beauty and there is something to be said for leaving certain wrecks so that others may have the chance to look later on. The divers gave us the skipper's lavatory pan – with the barnacles removed it would serve us well, if we ever had enough water.

The skin divers' descriptions of the wonderful things that they had seen on the ocean floor filled me with envy and I longed to go down to have a look for myself. They wanted to let me use one of their wet suits and breathing equipment but at my age without training the increasing pressures on the chest wall could be serious or even fatal. Instead I got hold of a mask, snorkel and flippers. Very soon I discovered the incredible beauty of the underwater world in those clear Hebridean seas, simply by floating on the surface and occasionally diving down a little way. It was fascinating to look at the forests of seaweeds, the crabs and clams moving about on the sand, and the small fish inquisitively nosing around my outstretched fingers. Those northern waters were very cold. Even on a hot summer's day and despite the warm currents of the Gulf Stream, it is impossible to float around for much longer than half an hour. One day I planned to invest in a wet suit to keep warmer – but I never did!

Philip Street, in the introduction to his book *Between the Tides* wrote, 'The seashore is a naturalist's paradise. Nowhere else in such a small area can he find so many animals of so many different types. Anyone interested in animals can probably learn more about animal life during a fortnight's holiday by the sea than during the rest of the year at home.'[1]

During the early days at Port na Luing all our efforts were directed at making the house watertight and comfortable. We were well aware that in our remote situation on the edge of the Atlantic it was a naturalist's paradise, but it was not until our third or fourth holiday that we had any time to make note of the living things around us. We soon realised that we were in the middle of a bird sanctuary, where, during the nesting season, we had to tread warily lest we stepped on the nests of gulls, terns, shell drake and many other birds. Wherever possible we made detailed notes of the nests and mapped their position on a large-scale plan. We also took photographs of the nests and eggs with a close-up lens. All skeletal remains of birds were collected and we hoped in time to have a skull representing every sort of bird, which visited Coll.

The incident with Guy's yacht and my inability to communicate with anyone had quite an effect on my life. Back at home I talked to a friend who was a radio amateur of long standing. He told me how to prepare for the Radio Amateurs' Examination and how I would have to be able to send and receive Morse code at 12 words per minute. I didn't have any trouble in passing the theory exam. However, when it came to learning the Morse, oh dear, oh dear! Doreen and the children put up with the noise of my Morse key every evening. I failed the exam twice, but after a year a very sympathetic operator from a marine radio station examined me. He quite literally pushed me through and a few weeks later I was the proud owner of the call sign G4FPP.

I obtained an instrument that was a combined receiver and transmitter called a transceiver. It was some time before I could take it up to Coll and I was a bit upset when I arrived at the village to see the new telephone link aerial on the hill behind the village. My radio services in an emergency would certainly not be required!

Down at Port na Luing I lost no time in fixing an aerial across our harbour. I parked the Land Rover in front of the house and kept the engine running while I connected my wireless to the battery. I sent out 'CQ' which means, 'Will someone speak to me please?' At once a very powerful signal came in. It was a radio ham only a few miles away called Tom; he, his wife Elsie and family had been holidaying on Coll for many years. Tom had been in the Royal Signals during the war and, under his expert guidance, I put up all manner of aerials around the house. He and his family became very good friends and regular visitors to Port na Luing. We often stayed with them in Edinburgh.

Most Sundays I called a number of hams in the Salisbury area. I was always in much demand by the Worked-all-Britain (WAB) amateurs, who attempted to make radio contact with all the rating squares in the UK. These are rather like postal codes and, with few amateurs visiting Coll; a radio contact with me was quite a prize!

One of my most interesting adventures in amateur radio came about one summer evening when the yacht 'Lucinda' sent out a maritime mobile signal. The skipper, Peter Aitchinson, explained that he was with his wife Caryl and their children on the other side of Tiree. He asked if I knew of a safe anchorage. I didn't but advised him to sail for Coll where we would be happy to look after the family. By the time he was in the Gunna Sound he radioed asking which side of a buoy he should steer. I had no idea, but a sailing ham from Oban broke in and said, 'Tell him to go to port.' I told Peter I would come out in our rowing boat and signal him by torchlight. I had forgotten that the boat was moored some 20 feet from the beach. It was high tide and I had to swim for it with the torch in my mouth. Fortunately it was a warm evening and I soon spotted Lucinda's navigation lights. I flashed my torch and was relieved when it was quickly acknowledged. Soon they had dropped anchor and I was rowing them all ashore with Caryl clutching a cooked chicken.

They turned out to be a delightful family who had recently sailed to America and knew one of my radio friends very well. The ladies prepared a super supper and then Peter went back to the yacht while the family spent the night with us. They became regular visitors to Port na Luing and once took Diana to Barra. A gale blew up – the first she had ever experienced in a small boat. She was not frightened, as the skipper and crew remained calm and cheerful all the time.

Later, Diana who was then teaching decided that she too would become a radio amateur. She passed the theory exam with no trouble and passed the Morse test first time!

1   Philip Street *Between the Tides* Philosophical Library Inc. 1953

9

Windmills and Lights

Once when I was a very small boy I stayed in a house by Loch Ard. I remember particularly a dam on the hillside full of little brown trout, which I caught in a net. Having watched them swim about in an oversized sweet jar, I returned them to the pool. Several hundred yards down the hill was an engine shed, which was the home of a water turbine and dynamo supplying the house with electricity. There was magic here for any boy, with the gurgling of the water, the hum of the dynamo and the impressive marble control panel consisting of knife switches, brass terminals and meters.

Whoever installed the apparatus must have been a genius because at night time, when more and more electric lights were turned on, it was possible to increase the speed of the dynamo by pulling a wire which ran from the porch to the engine shed. It caused a sluice gate to open and a greater flow of water to enter the turbine. I would eagerly wait until the lights became dim and then run out and pull on the wire. In a few moments, if the night was quiet, I was able to hear the increasing noise of the generator and watch the lights become brighter.

All that was many years ago and ever since I have always wanted to possess my own water generator. So I was rather disappointed to find that at Port na Luing the streams which flowed down from the hill into the sea were hardly ever more than a trickle of water. In high summer they dried up completely.

Mr Patmore at Acha Farm showed me his Lucas Freelite wind generator. It had been in almost constant operation for 20 years during which time it had charged many of the accumulators on the island and provided electric light for his home. I discovered that the equipment was no longer being made. Moreover wind generators never became popular because there was usually not enough wind to keep the accumulator fully charged. A 12-volt car headlight bulb took a lot of current and in return did not give very satisfactory domestic lighting. On Coll, however, there was nearly always some wind and 12-volt transistorised strip lights for caravans and yachts, which gave a high light output in return for their power consumption, had recently appeared. Since I could not use water I was determined to try the wind. An advertisement in that remarkable journal *Exchange and Mart* quickly put me in touch with a gentleman near Canterbury, who sold the entire equipment except for the control panel.

We sent most of the equipment up by rail but took the precious six-foot wind blade on the roof rack of the car. As so often seems to happen when you are searching for something unusual, we quite by chance found a fine unwanted control panel, which was mounted on the wall of a friend's house in Devon. She kindly presented it to us.

The obvious place to install the wind generator was upon the little hill to the west of the house where the uninhibited Atlantic winds came whistling in. The boys and I dug a hole on the summit and found solid rock about three feet down. We concreted into the hole a 14-foot long flooring joist, which we had stripped out of the house. It was made secure with guy wires. The tail fin was painted red and upon it in large letters we wrote 'Coll Electricity Co'. A few days later my old friend Hugh arrived. He was the Physician in Charge of the Physical Medicine Department in the hospital and by the nature of his work was particularly knowledgeable about electrical apparatus. We soon ran 100 feet of thick power line from the windmill mast to the control panel in our porch and connected it up to two six-volt ex-army tank accumulators and four strip lights. Having checked all the connections we screwed on the windmill blade, whereupon the wind suddenly dropped and nothing at all happened. After a maddening wait, by 10 o'clock that night it began blowing up to gale force. The revolutions of the windmill blade looked terrific in the half moonlight, the mast trembled with its vibrations, and the whine sounded rather like an aeroplane propeller. Back in the porch we had the immense satisfaction of seeing the ammeter needle at maximum charge. Soon we heard the wonderful sound of bubbles of gas coming out of the accumulators. The strip lights dazzled us at first and made the paraffin lamps look pathetic. My boyhood ambition to generate my own electricity had been realised at last!

Within two years of our initial triumph, we had put in 12 strip lights, which gave all the light that we required. Visitors sometimes remarked that they looked a bit out of place in such an isolated house on the edge of the Atlantic. Perhaps they did seem to be rather incongruous but they gave us an abundance of light whenever we wanted it. Our generator only failed us once in the summer of 1968. We all scorched and fried in the sun; the wind became a whisper and then disappeared altogether. We were able to cut down on the Calor Gas bill. When the children were by themselves in the house we had the satisfaction of knowing that the fire hazard was considerably reduced. I must admit, however, that when we returned at dusk after a day's fishing there was nothing quite so nice as the old paraffin lamp in a bedroom window to guide us into our little harbour.

Fired with enthusiasm after our initial success in producing free electric light, we put in a rotary converter, which gave a 240 volt DC supply from the two six volt accumulators. This was particularly useful because it enabled me to use a mains electric razor. We tried connecting it up to an electric blanket. At first we were rather disappointed. Although the bed became warm, it was never as hot and comfortable as with a proper mains supply. It occurred to me that we might obtain more heat by connecting the rotary converter directly to the wind generator. We went to bed and at first nothing much happened. In the early hours of the morning the wind blew up to gale force, the generator produced more and more power, the converter went

Coll Electricity Co. powers the house.

round faster and faster, and the electric blanket became hotter and hotter. Doreen and I both suddenly woke up at the same time and, with backsides almost aflame, leapt out of bed. This was an interesting experiment, which had most certainly worked but has never been repeated!

Years ago someone wrote an article in one of the popular science magazines advocating the use of giant wind generators in the north of Scotland. It claimed that they could provide a significant quota of power to the national grid, especially in the winter when the orthodox generating stations were working to full capacity and were sometimes overloaded. The author illustrated his article with interesting and convincing diagrams. Nothing more was heard of these schemes until recently when wind farms began appearing. Credit must be given to the French, who developed and perfected water turbines driven by the enormous forces of the tidal flow. One wonders if the electricity authorities in this country could not do still more to harness our own natural resources of potential electric power. On the one hand we have power stations fired by the fossil fuels, oil, gas and coal, and, on the other, super sophisticated and fantastically expensive nuclear reactors. Could we not exploit our hydroelectric resources and give more consideration to the tremendous potential of the tides, wind and the sun?

I must confess that I have become a bit obsessional about windmills and never miss the chance of looking closely at the building and its mechanism whenever the chance presents itself. Only a few remain operational. A great many are derelict and falling to pieces; heaven knows how many have disintegrated without trace.

Years before we found Coll, we visited Craster on the Northumberland coast. There we saw in someone's front garden a fantastic collection of miniature windmills with sails turning in the wind. Among this remarkable assembly was a little veteran car mounted on top of a pole; a small propeller caused a diminutive articulated man with a top hat to crank away at the starting handle. The greater the force of the wind the faster did the wee man apply himself to his task. This childish mechanism appealed to my simple mind enormously. When I have time I plan to make a number of wind-driven models and to install them on the pit prop posts holding the fence in front of Port na Luing. So far I have only carved out a few 12-inch wooden propellers but I have drawn up plans for little wind-driven men riding bicycles, sawing wood and pumping water. Perhaps the best scheme of all would be to make models of existing and vanished windmills and watch their gorgeous sails turning in the wind.

10

The Coll Show and a Wedding

Every August the Coll Horticultural Society holds it annual show. Very occasionally a couple on the island get married so there is a wedding as well. Once both these functions occurred during the same holiday in 1969.

Alec and Flora's two daughters were married within 12 months of each other and we were invited to the second wedding when Margaret married John Wheeler James. The ceremony commenced at 6.30 in the evening so that everyone could get the cows milked and the day's work on the farm finished. Many people arrived early and the church was pretty full by the time we got there. Soon the pews were packed. Over 200 filled the building with the children standing at the back. Everyone was dressed in their best. The ladies' hats and dresses would have done credit to any society function. Nurse, who always played the harmonium, tried to lift the lid of the instrument but found that it was locked. Big Archie came to the rescue and was able to reach the key from its hiding place above the hymn board. She gave an excellent rendering of Bach's 'Jesu, Joy of Man's Desiring', but gave up when Mr Cowie, the gamekeeper, produced an air on his pipes in the porch to announce the bride's arrival. A few minutes later the smiling congregation were delighted to see her walking down the aisle on her father's arm. After a short service the visiting minister delivered the blessing in Gaelic. It was one of the most impressive things I have ever heard.

Outside the church everyone seemed to produce a camera. Some were ancient box contrivances, which probably hadn't seen the light of day for years. However, the professional had all the latest electronic flash things hanging round his neck. His kilt and matching tie made him look a bit like a Christmas tree. Soon he had the couple, parents, bridesmaids and guests assembled with Eatharna Bay in the background. It was a cool evening with a fair wind blowing, but all concerned laughed and smiled for nearly half an hour as the amateurs and the professional took their photographs.

The newlyweds were smothered with confetti and climbed into a Dormobile, which headed the procession to the village hall half a mile away. Many followed on foot and at the end were several cars and the Land Rovers, including our own. A few hundred yards from the hall the bridal party alighted and the procession continued on foot led by the piper.

On the stage of the hall there was a high table with the minister presiding. Others sat at tables in the body of the hall. We were presented with a magnificent feast with numerous toasts taken in unadulterated whisky. Not a few supplemented their quota with their own private supply. After the feast there were speeches and more toasts. It was 10 o'clock by the time everyone began to clear the hall to make ready for the dance. We were quite casually told that this would continue throughout the night until the ferry-boat arrived. In fact it was not very long ago that Coll dances would go on for several days and nights with dancers coming in relays. It was quite a thing to watch the men's hobnail boots striking sparks on the concrete floor.

Everyone danced with everyone. There were no sad wallflowers sitting out vainly waiting for a partner. It became hotter and hotter, and soon coats were off. The bride in her wedding gown looked serenely happy as she danced with her guests. The piper, who alternated with two accordionists and a lady playing a plastic box device activated by means of an electronic pencil, provided music. All three instruments were connected by cables to large black trunks labelled 'Vox', from which issued a tremendous noise. I preferred the piper.

In the early hours I helped Hughie, the local registrar, load his Dormobile with crates and crockery. In the road outside the hall we met a number of guests taking wee drams. I must have had about half a pint of undiluted firewater before we got going. By the time we arrived at Hughie's house and pushed the crates of crockery under a bed I found that my voice was croaking. Hughie assured me that all I needed was another dram. I knocked it back and discovered that I had no voice at all. Back at the hall it was by way of sign language that I was able to explain my predicament to Doreen and that I felt it was about time we went back to Port na Luing. Later we heard that the ferry-boat did not get in until 8 am and that many stalwarts had spent the night dancing so as to be on the pier to see the bride and groom off on their honeymoon.

A few days after the wedding the 48th Annual Coll Show took place. For several years I had heard about it months before when the Laird's mother-in-law had sent me a request for a donation, but so far we had always missed this function. Entries had to be assembled by 10.30 on the morning of the event. Diana made a model of the Loch Ness Monster out of limpet shells and Dorothy Anne an abstract arrangement in which the shells were painted with nail polish; they both won a second prize. David had made a miniature garden in the base of an empty pie tin, but knocked it over on the way to the village. However he won first prize for a bedside locker he had made. Doreen gained a second for a knitted jersey and I was given a third for a table, which was no great achievement since it was the only entry in the adult carpentry class. It took quite a time to arrange our exhibits. While we were doing so Doreen dropped a clanger; she saw a plate of meringues and said to a lady standing nearby, 'If I had known that the standard was so low I would certainly have made some meringues.' The lady smiled sweetly and said, 'As a matter of fact I made them.' She won the first prize.

At first sight the exhibits looked like those we had seen so often in the marquees on summer Saturday afternoons in a number of Wiltshire and Hampshire villages, but on closer examination there were things that were different. The vegetables were of a good size and well grown, but for the most part not very well presented. There were few knitted garments and a very poor showing of home baked scones and cakes. The only exhibit in the adult carpentry class was my own miserable effort. As is so often the case, the children's sections of handicrafts, miniature gardens, wild flowers and seashell arrangements showed originality, which put them in a class above their parents. I was surprised to see no section for homemade wines.

Outside in the sunshine the events were much more cheerful. Many of the men, and some of the women, were dressed in the kilt, and very colourful they looked. I was fascinated to note that some men wore their kilts so that their knees were discreetly hidden, but others favoured a sort of mini garment, which stopped halfway down the thigh. The entire gathering of several hundred was dominated by an enormously large, cheerful, kilted cleric, smoking a Sherlock Holmes pipe and leaning on a shepherd's crook. They called him 'The Bishop'. He, together with members of the Tiree pipe band and others, could be seen from time to time propping up the temporary bar at the back of the hall drinking beer, whisky or both. After the night of the wedding the week before, I was unable to face anything stronger than tea.

The children, expertly trained by Chrissie at the school, gave an excellent display of Scottish dancing to the tune of Mr Cowie's pipes. Others took part in long and high jump competitions or ran races, had pony rides, drank Coca Cola through straws, and ate potato chips. There was supposed to be a sheep dog competition but there was not a single entry. Some years ago they had abandoned the outboard motor races on the Loch since there were so few boats. One solitary man played darts and it was not until I spotted the leather strap sticking out of his right hand trouser pocket that I realised he was a policeman without his tunic or cap. Nobody really knows why a member of the law always comes over to the Coll Show; perhaps someone once drank too much and went berserk.

After tea the prizes were presented. One of the judges delivered a forthright but tactful speech in which she decried the fact that on such a lovely island as Coll she had only been asked to judge three gardens. She was saddened that the home baking class had been so poorly supported. She could only hope that this was because most housewives were exhausted after the wedding. There followed a rather lengthy speech by a gentleman who had judged the vegetables. He analysed and commented on almost every single specimen exhibited. Indeed, anyone interested enough could have acquired sufficient material from his observations, to write a useful compendium on vegetable growing.

The grand finale came with a tug of war match between the men of Coll and the visitors. All seemed to be going well until the very large cleric added his weight and the rope snapped. After it had been mended three times, they decided to call it a day and we all went home.

11

I Was Poisoned and Had Sick Leave

It wasn't really my fault that someone poured some concentrated chlorine solution into a half empty rainwater butt instead of a full one and then gave me a cup of tea brewed with the poison. As it so happened it was fortunate for the future of our house that my guts did odd things almost immediately. By the time I arrived home I fairly rapidly went into a sort of decline. The pain became so awful that I spent a part of September 1982 in hospital. I was X-rayed, investigated, prodded and probed, and fed nothing but milk and pills. After this I was solemnly told to take quiet sick leave for a fortnight and on no account exert myself in any way.

Doreen and I had never packed our bags so quickly. Within two hours of being discharged from hospital we were on our way and by teatime heading northwards up the M6. We reached Penrith in time for a meal at the Chinese restaurant and suddenly I had the wonderful feeling of being quite alright again. Next day we followed a delightful road from Gretna Green to Edinburgh, which passed by the origin of the Tweed, and spent the night at Aberfeldy. There had been several recent sightings of the Loch Ness Monster so we thought we would motor along General Wade's military road and have a look for ourselves. However the skies suddenly darkened and we reached Oban in torrential rain.

The ferry-boat banged against her moorings all night but she sailed on time. The wind eased up after Tobermory but it was still raining hard when we got ashore at Coll. Everywhere there were lakes of water and blocked field drains flooded the track down to the house. I thought it rather odd that we never got bogged down and never once did I have to put the Land Rover into four-wheel drive. I soon discovered the reason for this when I was digging a hole for a clothes' line pole; the first few inches of soil were saturated but the underlying peat was bone dry. It seemed that the subsoil everywhere on the island was failing to absorb any water after the prolonged drought of the previous summer.

It went on raining continuously for several days. On the first Sunday the only living things we saw were a few gulls and a very bedraggled looking otter running over the rocks by the jetty. In the evening Doreen opened the valve of the chemical toilet, which drained the contents into a soak away. She remarked that it seemed to be emptying very slowly. On our way to bed we noticed hairline cracks appearing in the concrete floor in the drawing room, which were wet and oozing.

Neither of us could get to sleep so after a while I went down to investigate. I couldn't at first find the light switch and suddenly realised that my

feet were wet. I lit a match and saw almost four inches of water in the drawing room. The hall was also awash and when I opened the bathroom door an
empty hot water bottled floated through. The front porch was still dry and
the accumulators were giving plenty of power. The water was rising fairly
rapidly and in the drawing room a fish box was now afloat and steam was
coming off the legs of the hot stove.

There was a strong wind blowing and it was raining fairly hard. However
it wasn't particularly cold. A half moon appeared from behind the clouds
and between the back of the house and the hillside we saw a lake of water
with several streams pouring into it from the rocky plateau above. The well
and water tanks were overflowing and adding to the deluge.

There was only one thing to do and that was to dig trenches from the
growing lake at the back of the house into the sea as quickly as possible. I
started badly by puncturing the alkathene water pipe with a fork. The jet hit
me fair and square in the face. We both soon had water coming over the top
of our gumboots. Almost until daybreak we squelched about digging for all
we were worth. A few yards from the sea we came across a great rock, which
we couldn't budge and had to dig several yards round it. At last by torchlight we saw fresh water pouring onto the beach and making a pond in the
sand. In spite of the noise of the wind and the waves, we could just hear the
sound of running water pouring down the ditch; it sounded like music!

The water level had gone down a little in the drawing room and hall but
we didn't fancy the idea of mopping it up with floor cloths. I remembered
that some of the rocks in the wall beneath the new window were loose. We
levered several out with the poker and made a hole at floor level to the outside. With brooms we eventually managed to sweep out most of the water,
relit the fire, and went to bed.

It was well into the afternoon when we woke up. The floor downstairs
was practically dry and the lake had disappeared. Water was still pouring
down the hillside. To be safe we reckoned we must dig down a further two
feet and put in drain pipes. Fortunately Alastair at the Hotel had an assort-
ment of old pipes, which he gave to us the following morning. Henry and
his wife, Kitty, appeared for a quiet holiday. We had thought of 'phoning
and asking them not to come, but they had looked forward to their visit so
much and optimistically. We just hoped that the water level would stop rising and our friends wouldn't find a week at Port na Luing too awful. In fact
they were obviously delighted to find that there was plenty of work to do.
Although Henry had been retired as a Consultant Physician for several
years he gave the impression that he had been a professional drain layer all
his life. When their son Joe joined us, we soon had drains radiating from all
angles at the back of the house running into the sea. As always Jimmy came
to our rescue with his tractor and hauled out the rock, which had diverted
the direct flow. He and Margaret stayed for supper and it was dark when
they left on the tractor. Henry, at that time, was Senior Magistrate on the
Salisbury Bench. He smiled and said, 'If Jimmy was before me I could have
got him for being unlicensed, uninsured, never having passed a driving

Tom Dickson finds dowsing does not work if you have a metal bucket over your head.

test, having a vehicle at night with no lights and carrying a passenger on a tractor!'

In the garage in Oban, when I started the car up for the trip back south, I realised how wonderfully well and relaxed I felt. It had certainly been a successful sick leave!

Drains and water were the main topic of conversation on the journey home . . .

In the early days we carried water from a spring about 150 feet from the house. We were fortunate to have found a wooden yoke that fitted on to the shoulders. With a chain attached to each end it was a helpful, if somewhat uncomfortable way of carrying the precious fluid. When you consider the hundreds of gallons of water a family can get through each day, it was amazing how little we managed with. One eggcup full was the usual ration for cleaning teeth!

It was clear that we would have to do something to improve our water supply. Rainwater collected in butts was not going to be sufficient. Alec and Flora told us about how once, when they were desperately short of water, they had called in a water dowser. He had quickly found a stream just a few feet under the ground and close to their house. On one holiday Tom and I decided that we would try our hand at water divining ourselves. How dowsing works remains a mystery. It would appear that a larger movement of pendulum, rods, or other device detects slight movements of the arm muscles. We used metal coat hanger wire cut into an L shape, which we held loosely in each fist, parallel to the ground. We were quite encouraged when we independently obtained readings over the same area.

I read somewhere that there is a very minute deposit of iron in the skull, somewhere near to the ears. We tried dowsing in areas where we had already detected water, but this time we put metal buckets over our heads. We obtained no reaction at all. We changed to plastic buckets and immediately got positive results. During this experiment a party of visitors walked nearby and promptly disappeared over the hill!

We realised that because of the numerous rocks we could never dig out efficient drains into the sea. Two professional drain diggers were working on the island so we persuaded them to come down to us. They were a delightful Irish couple. 'Half the lies he tells aren't true', one said of his mate. They had with them a roll of wire, fuses and a biscuit tin containing sticks of gelignite, which had been used in building the new pier. The sticks looked like a very runny Brie cheese and could obviously be lethal. The men dug the gelignite into strategic positions and Stephen connected the wire to the Land Rover battery, parked up the drive. Soon there were proper trenches and pipes were laid. It is much to their credit that all the explosions broke only one window.

12

The Last Chapter

When I retired about 25 years ago I became very involved in making dolls' houses and miniature furniture in the style of Charles Rennie Mackintosh, as a result the writing of this book was abandoned. The Salisbury harpsichord maker, Jim Mogford, persuaded me to join him in making a substantial model of Salisbury Cathedral under construction. The model was well received and is now on view in that splendid building.

At last we were able to go to Coll for months rather than weeks. It is interesting to look back and note the changes on the island during the last quarter of a century. I am now 80 years of age and becoming increasingly infirm both physically and mentally. In fact I am going quite potty. I am concerned that if I don't finish the book off now it will be too late!

The weathermen say it is becoming warmer but I haven't noticed it. I don't doubt that the tides are getting higher as the icecaps melt. However the pattern of lovely days followed by a battering gale is unchanged.

One of the most important things that happened is that Diana married a splendid chap called Pete – her choice of husband was shrewd because he is a builder and loves Port na Luing! Neither he nor anyone else will ever finish the house. Gales frequently bash the building and paintwork. Our children and their families' holidays in Coll are still dominated by ongoing maintenance and repairs to the building.

My eldest daughter, Dorothy, her husband Bill and their two daughters Marion and Kathryn continue to love Coll and regularly holiday there. The girls have now reached an age when they can visit with friends. They both seem to be much more sensible than our own children were at that age, so no sleepless nights worrying about what they are up to and how the house is surviving! Stephen married a charming girl called Vanessa and produced a lively wee boy called Archie. Both enjoy the freedom of Coll and would love to be able to spend more time there.

The old folk: Mrs Hinkson, Jimmy and Margaret, Alec and Flora, and many more have all gone, and, alas, some younger people as well. A new generation is coming to Coll. The population has increased to about 150 and there are about 20 children in the thriving village school.

The Laird, Ken Stewart, was taken ill and went to the Lowlands with his family where he is farming again. It seems strange to have no resident laird! Their house, Acha, is a holiday home, but Janet Stewart still owns Stronvar where we first stayed during that very cold building holiday.

Mains electricity eventually came to the island. Everyone was offered installation at a very reasonable rate and few refused it. My enthusiasm for the

Freelite wind generator eventually waned. It's output was very limited and was utterly dependent on the wind. We have three quarters of a mile of poles to bring the overhead cables to the house – heaven knows how much it would cost to install today! At first the power came by undersea cable from two old RAF generators on Tiree. We, being far west were nearly the first to have mains electricity and it was nearly a year before the rest of the island was connected. In those early days, folk would often come down to see the wonders of 'the electric' in our house!

With mains electricity came the use of power tools, making much of the rebuilding work easier and faster. In the early days of electric power from Tiree, we often got mini power cuts, lasting for several minutes and sometimes longer, due to the engineer's delay in switching the ancient generators

We had always cooked with the Calor gas stove and, when the electricity came, a Baby Belling. A few years ago an islander ordered a state of the art Calor gas range. An electric model was delivered by mistake. Rather than have the heavy thing transported back to the mainland we bought it. With it's double oven and other extras we're now really cooking at Port na Luing!

The family wanted more mod cons. A shower was installed in the bathroom. Diana, insisting she would not wash clothes by hand, bought a washing machine. A friend gave us a small bore loo, (excellent when you have to put pipes through two feet thick walls!), which has been installed, in a newly built 'smallest room' at one end of the middle bedroom. We christened the appliance 'the grinder' after the extraordinary noise it makes. No one is allowed to flush it at night! Stephen acquired a splendid ship's porthole, which allows light in from the interior wall. All of these things are fine, but completely useless if there is no water to service them!

It is very sad to relate that the bitumen membrane I had so patiently applied to the roof eventually perished and fell to pieces. There was nothing I could do but get contractors, then on the island, to put on a corrugated asbestos structure. Now that time has weathered it and there are lichens growing, it doesn't look too bad. We console ourselves with the knowledge that we are not rained upon at night and that the roof is no longer a fire hazard!

As Doreen and I have got more and more groggy, our children insisted that in spite of my amateur radio, we should have a telephone installed. Eventually, over a mile of cable was dug into the ground from Breachacha. The dreadful machine works well, but just occasionally the cable gets ploughed up and Port na Luing is again a haven from the dreaded bells. The family all use mobile 'phones but I am quite happy to remain blissfully ignorant about them.

We put down a wooden floor in the drawing room and even covered it in linoleum. The Jøtul stove eventually rusted and Tom and I built a replacement with Coll stone. It works quite well, but like all others it smokes when the wind is from the north. Somehow Stephen got hold of a nice staircase with a strong banister. He took it to Coll on a roof rack. It now replaces my original pine model, is wider and less steep . . . much easier on my ageing legs!

Our grandson Archie is approaching five years old. He loves to help with jobs in the house and knows the names of most of the tools, though he does have a tendency to hide them! Recently, he was taken on holiday to Spain, but announced that he would much rather be at his 'beach house'!

Pete finished the porch and put down a carpet. I made a sofa out of massive drift wood planks. It's fine, except that it is too heavy to move!

In the past 25 years many island houses have been improved, or, like Port na Luing, rescued from complete ruination.

Before we discovered Coll, Guy and Jean Jardine occupied the remote house at the end of Crossapol Bay. Guy was good at basic carpentry and always claimed that rusty nails were better than new ones! He made a successful room especially for his charts but had less luck with a greenhouse kit he ordered from the mainland. The wee building was duly erected against a south-facing wall. All went well until one day a visitor went to inspect. He thought that the door opened inwards when in fact it opened outwards. He gave it a shove and nothing happened . . . he shoved harder and the entire building collapsed in a shower of splintered wood, broken glass, Jean's precious plants and smashed flower pots!

Guy and Jean moved to the village. Ronnie and Mairi Hedderwick and their two children lived in Crossapol House for a few years and founded The Malin workshop. Mairi's beautiful illustrations were used on a huge variety of cards, notepaper and calendars and sold all over Scotland. They moved to Fort William and the house changed hands again. John Sharpley, a GP from the Cotswolds, and his wife Elizabeth moved in. He often did locums for the resident doctor and was very keen on fishing and lobstering. Once he decided to take quite a large party over to the small island of Gunna. He planned to make two trips. Doreen went with the first party and getting out of the boat promptly fell in, but she found the water quite warm. I waited with the others on Coll. When John came back to collect us he couldn't get the outboard to start again. He took the plug out and managed to dry it with a cigarette lighter. The motor spluttered erratically to life and slowly but surely we made our way to Gunna. We were not going to risk two more journeys and everyone clambered into the small boat for the return journey! Although the sea was calm, the boat was so overloaded that the sea was nearly over the gunwales. . . we were all extremely wet by the time we got back, relieved, to Crossapol. A few years later we were very sad when the Sharpleys eventually gave up their holiday home.

To our delight Mairi Hedderwick moved back to Crossapol. She had become well known for her delightful books about the adventures of Katie Morag on the island of Struay. The fictional island bears a great resemblance to Coll and it is wonderful to see the similarity between some of Struay's inhabitants and some of the (sadly gone) old Collachs. Mairi gives talks to schoolchildren on the mainland and has made several appearances on the television, which has certainly put Coll on the map. It is not unusual to see visiting children looking for Katie Morag!

George Walker & Sons fish boxes were amongst my favourites for furniture making.

Mairi kept hens, made a duck pond and had a superb kitchen garden manured with kelp. We all remember her parties! We were desperately sad when Mairi moved back to the mainland. Crossapol house now belongs to a delightful couple from Glasgow.

Chris and Tessa Facey rescued most expertly Walkers Cottage at Breachacha Farm from dereliction. It is a charming wee place with one bedroom, a sitting room, bathroom and tiny kitchen. They re-tiled the roof, plumbed it and put in mains electricity. Chris had been an electrician on the mainland. One summer, Diana and Tessa swapped husbands each day for a week or so. Pete plastered and tiled the bathroom at Walker's and Chris expertly replaced the rather awful wiring that David and I had done some time previously. He put in the sockets at waist height. When you think about it, it really is rather daft to bend double to plug in any appliance! Chris replaced the old wire fuses with the latest circuit breakers, which, I am told, act so quickly in the case of a short circuit that the electric shock is too rapid to electrocute!

Whilst we all admired Chris's electrical installations, we could never say the same about his seamanship . . . it was absolutely terrible! He had a small plastic boat with an outboard motor. Virtually every time he came into our harbour he hit the same rock and broke the shearing pin, which protects the propeller. We had to keep a stock of bits of aluminium rod to repair the engine!

Tessa was a jolly good cook and baked the most wonderful bread I have ever tasted. Her loaves always contain plenty of roughage and keep one nice and regular! She is also very artistic and her stencilling and carvings were in much demand. Once she showed me a massive water-colour brush called the 'Ron Ranson Hake' and got quite cross when I told her it would be ideal for painting window frames!

They had an extensive, well chosen collection of books that, in their fish boxes, filled an entire wall of their sitting room. We nearly cried when they told us they were leaving Coll to live in the warmer climate of Menorca. We have their very comfortable double bed and fine kitchen table at Port na Luing and still miss them dreadfully.

At Bousd, Wil and Jonathan Tunnell re-built one of the finest cottages on the island. The foundations were little more than a few stones and it took them quite a while to finish the job. Much of the furniture they made from driftwood, just as John Barr at Hyne had done, so many years before. In the village the Smiths have most expertly rebuilt the Old Smithy.

Big Archie had been on Coll for many years. He was well named, as he seemed to be the tallest man on the island. He was once a policeman in Glasgow, a Sergeant I think. He was much respected and an important official in the Wee Free Church. On one memorable and horrific occasion we attended a funeral that he and the minister were conducting. It was quite a simple affair. Archie was giving a blessing in Gaelic with his strong voice. He lifted his arms above his head, which made him appear over eight feet high. Then, with a terrible crash, he fell down. No one could see his body because it lay behind a short screen. I was pretty sure he had dropped dead. The congregation were in a state of turmoil and shock. The minister was speechless and seemed quite helpless. To try and pacify everyone I looked over the screen and said, 'What are you up to Archie?' However, when I examined the body on the floor it had all the signs of death. I told the minister that it might be as well to conclude the service outside, which he did.

It was the custom to take a body back home, but I persuaded them to leave it in the place he loved so much. A coffin arrived a few days later, so that week there were two internments in the cemetery. With Big Archie gone the church ceased to function, which was a shame.

The island has seen a variety of enterprises over the years. The most important, employing a number of people, must be Project Trust. At about the same time as we started to rebuild Port na Luing, Major Nicholas Maclean Bristol and his wife Lavinia resurrected the old castle at Breachacha and founded the charity. The Project selects and trains students before sending them to a variety of countries around the world, during their gap year, before University. The students do a whole range of jobs including teaching, farming and building. Project Trust has grown from strength to strength and has rebuilt and enlarged Bally Haugh house to make a splendid head-quarters and conference centre. It was a great day for Coll when HRH Prince Charles visited the centre and the school. He met a great number of Collachs but hadn't reckoned on the enthusiasm of Katie Sproat. She grasped him firmly with both hands and would not let go – this put the tight schedule back by several minutes!

Alastair who ran the hotel when we first arrived passed the hotel onto his son Kevin and daughter-in-law Julie who have extended the hotel. It is not unusual for yachts to detour to Coll, or for folk to make a special trip from Tiree for the excellent cuisine. Julie is self-taught and has developed a mouth-watering array of dishes, many of which use local ingredients.

The Coll Hotel, courtesy of Julie Oliphant.

Brian and Fra opened 'The First Port of Coll', an excellent restaurant in the village. Kip and Carole set up a studio and gift shop, 'The Lighthouse', behind the hotel. Kip paints excellent watercolour views of the island and Carole creates beautiful pictures on fabric. Both are extremely popular with visitors and islanders.

Fiona and Angus Kennedy took over the Post Master's wee house next to the post office. They sell an incredible collection of artefacts and local crafts in their shop 'An Acarsaid'.

Wendy McKechnie set up an enterprising business 'Coll Herbals', making a great variety of herbal cosmetics. The business took over the old hostel in the village and for many years employed several people. Today Wendy makes specialist lotions for individuals.

Shops have come and gone over the years. Now there is only one run by Neal and Shirley. It is well stocked and very welcoming. Neal makes regular visits to the mainland and is always happy to seek out any special requirements you may have. Several people on the island make excellent produce for sale, including delicious goats' cheese, chutneys and preserves.

There are now several Bed and Breakfasts on the island. Robert and Ruth Sturgeon built a splendid guesthouse with magnificent views across the sea. Robert used to take their guests out fishing in his boat and the same folk returned year after year. Robert and Ruth were a delightful couple. We were

The Craft Shop, courtesy of Fiona Kennedy.

all deeply shocked when Robert dropped dead watching Scotland play Brazil in the 1998 World Cup.

In 1995, hard working enthusiasts constructed a nine-hole golf course at Cliad. Cow pats, sheep and rabbits make challenging hazards and, at times, flag poles are broken by the cattle. Islanders and visitors make good use of the course and there are regular matches, rewarded by a number of trophies.

A new fire station has been built in the village. It is certainly not a thing of beauty, but the splendid Strathclyde Fire Engine is the very latest. It is manned entirely by volunteers with Kevin from the hotel in charge. There is a weekly practice and sometimes they come down to Port na Luing on exercise. On one occasion the sound of sirens and the sight of flashing blue lights alerted us to their arrival. The crew leapt out of the engine, all wearing breathing apparatus and came in for refreshment. I could barely recognise any of them in their costumes, but as they removed the apparatus I realised that one was a beautiful girl! She flung her arms around me and gave me a lovely kiss. I don't remember her name, but I will never forget her embrace!

A number of doctors have come and gone since we first discovered Coll. During the first few days of one holiday the resident GP suffered a heart attack. I was called to help and had to arrange to have him flown off the island. I was then left as locum for the island. I remember particularly a boy who complained of violent abdominal pain. I could find nothing at all the matter with him. His mother told me that he was due to go back to school in

Oban in a few days time. I told her that she must keep him in a darkened room with nothing to eat but cold porridge. He very soon recovered!

We knew Dr Gill De Mornay best of all. She had an ancient camera with which she took superb photographs of birds and, in particular, corncrakes. She had a passion for two enormous dogs and a minute chiaouaoa. She was a first rate table-tennis player and was well known for beating anyone who had the temerity to challenge her!

Dr Gill retired to the mainland. She still has three dogs and we keep in touch by telephone, but sadly, never see her. Since her departure a new medical centre with facilities to rival any on the mainland has been built. It is well equipped with a dispensary, oxygen and anaesthetic equipment, none of which were present when we first visited Coll. There must be some good reason why there is no basic X-ray equipment. Urgent casualties used to be transported to the mainland by an aeroplane ambulance. Today a helicopter can arrive within an hour. Air ambulance nurses on board get their 'wings' after their first few flights. Once Diana was alone at Port na Luing and became acutely ill. Dr Gill had her flown to hospital in Glasgow. Within no time members of the splendid Coll Association, based in Glasgow, arrived at the hospital with flowers, magazines and offers of help. Dr Tony Thirsk was a very senior obstetrician and gynaecologist who often did locums for Dr Gill. He and his wife Josephine (a superb cook) became very good friends of ours and are always most welcome visitors.

When the Laird left Coll the Royal Society for the Protection of Birds bought much of his land and Port na Luing is now situated on the edge of a nature reserve. The prime purpose of their purchase was to protect and encourage the breeding of corncrakes. They introduced special farming methods on their land and encouraged farmers elsewhere on the island to adopt the same. Cat owners were asked to fit collars with bells on around their pets' necks to warn the birds of impending danger. Some feline fanatics did not think much of the idea! The whole thing has been a marked success with the number of corncrakes increasing annually. Coll has always been an ornithological heaven and now, with the added interest of the RSPB there are more birdie people visiting the island. Personally, although it is always thrilling to see a corncrake, I find the dreadful noise they make a confounded nuisance at night! Once a corncrake sadly killed itself on some wire netting. A Collach, who must remain nameless, cooked it and declared to me that it made very good eating!

In 1988 the author Pat Barr, then living at Hyne, together with Mairi Hedderwick, took a risk and launched *The Coll magazine*. In the second volume Pat wrote, 'When I first suggested starting this magazine two years ago a few pessimists said there was nothing worth writing about Coll and no-one to write it anyway. How wonderfully wrong they were!' Since then the magazine has come out annually packed with island news, articles by Collachs and 'summer swallows', tales of the island's history, nature notes and poems, stories and pictures by boys and girls of the school. There are delightful illustrations by Mairi Hedderwick, Kip Poulson and others in the magazines. In every issue there are several outstanding articles. For example, the 1997 edition contains 'A day in the life of a nature warden in Coll' by Charlie Self. I have read and enjoyed it several times.

Much later *Coll Information News* (CIN) was launched. Today, Emma Grant produces it each month. It is a most ambitious broad sheet with every scrap of island news. For example the 'Dates for your Diary' February 2002, includes events such as a drumming workshop, Education Forum meeting, the Hebridean Sheep Conference, as well as classes in languages and Tai Chi.

Martin Lunghi (alas now left the island) published an annual telephone directory in which all the subscribers are listed alphabetically, together with their Christian names. He listed people such as the Doctor and the police (on Tiree) under 'Emergency Numbers' and most helpfully, includes a section of 'Frequently used Numbers' which includes places such as the shop, pier and hotel. 'Moderately useful numbers' includes council services, banking information and mainland hospitals! Martin also wrote an excellent, informative and entertaining guide to Coll, and edited a cookbook.

On the first few occasions that we went to Coll we were transferred from the ferry-boat to the motor launch and landed at the old pier. At the time an army of engineers were blasting a road from the village to a site about half a mile away. In a few years the pier was completed to everyone's satisfaction. A substantial building was erected. It housed an office, cargo store, waiting room and toilets. Later the ferry service was enhanced by the addition of roll-on roll-off facilities. Getting a car to and from the island had become a relatively simple matter! John Wheeler James took over the job of pier master from Alec, his father-in-law.

It seemed to me that everything always worked very smoothly, but then an extraordinary thing happened. Caledonian MacBrayne abandoned the building and built a new office and waiting room. Many folk thought the whole thing was a terrible waste of money.

Something good came from all this however: Tammie, Mairi Hedderwick's daughter, took over the original building and converted it into a pottery, 'Coll Ceramics'. Tammie produces some excellent pieces. Her lessons are very popular with islanders and visitors alike. Tammie has to import her clay from the mainland but is hopeful that local sources she has been experimenting with will eventually provide all that she needs.

When they retired from farming, Alec and Flora left Arileod and moved to Kilbride. After they died Nic and Olvin bought the house and they converted the byre into a furniture workshop. Olvin calls himself a 'Bodger' – a Chiltern wood turner, he explains, making chair legs with a pole lathe for Windsor chairs. In his workshop he has the latest electric saws but his pole lathe dominates the place. It's well worth a visit to see it in operation. If he's not too busy ask him to show you the 50 feet long poly tunnel behind the house. There they grow the most splendid vegetables. Folk took bets on whether it would survive the first gale – several years later it's still standing and doing very well!

For a long time Erskine Beveridge's book, *Coll and Tiree: Their Prehistoric Forts and Ecclesiastical Antiquities With Notices of Ancient Remains in the Treshnish Isles*, has been the Archaeologists' Bible. Recently, a most enterprising 'Coll Archaeology Society' has been formed. Regular meetings are held and there are often visits from professionals. Frequent field trips have made exciting finds, including bronze age flints, the remains of stone circles, tools made from hornblende, ancient headstones and other features of burial grounds. Excellent aerial photographs have been made with a camera attached to a homemade radio controlled glider. A description of the society can be found in *The Coll Magazine* of 2002.

In the same magazine there is an account by Sheila McKinnon about breeding Eriskay and miniature palomino Shetland ponies on the island. Sheila has to be prepared to provide any veterinary services that are needed, and some of it is obviously pretty heroic! You can see the delightful ponies in the roadside fields as you drive from the village heading towards the west end.

Logan Air, based in Glasgow did, for a short while, operate regular flights to the Ballard airstrip. Often Allan Brodie had to clear his cows off the field and hoist a windsock before a landing could be made! There are ways of getting to Coll quickly. Pete regularly drives up with the dogs a week or so before term ends. Diana leaves Southampton airport about seven in the morning, spends a couple of hours at Glasgow airport, before getting a small plane to Tiree. From there a local fisherman brings her directly into the bay at Port na Luing in time for lunch! If you time it right, you can get from Tiree to London in three hours, but who wants to be in London anyway!

We must have had many hundred visitors at Port na Luing over the years, some staying, but most just calling in. Some known to us, and some complete strangers. Perhaps one of the most unusual visits was when a group of men dressed in oilskins, marched up the beach and announced, 'We've come for our chocolate cake'. Not wishing to argue, we told them it would be ready in a couple of hours. When they returned, armed with a crate of fish, the sun was shining and they joined us for a drink. Imagine their embarrassment, and our amusement when they told us that they had read in a skin divers' journal that they could exchange fish for chocolate cake at Port na Luing! It was the first we'd heard of it, but so started a happy few years of bartering!

The family have had all sorts of people to stay. The Pearson family were there for the eclipse in 1999. A cloudy disappointing event, brightened by the fluorescent cakes and biscuits that Laura and Sophie baked! Bruce, a wildlife artist, spent many happy hours in our boat, lying over the stern sketching seaweeds through the bottom of a floating glass dish! Whistling Willy spent almost an entire five days installing a water tank . . . I'm told his whistling inside the 1000-gallon tank was phenomenal! Sue enthusiastically researched mice and bats. She showed us how to make paper from flag iris leaves. The result was very good to look at but not too kind on my fountain pen nib!

In 2002, Argyll and Bute Council offered a free computer, printer and web camera to every permanent household on Coll, as well as to a number of other isolated communities. Directly, or indirectly, we are all dependent on these electronic marvels. Our children have 'lap top' devices. Once, when Diana was typing part of this book, she was visited by a 'virus', which, for a time, resulted in confusion and dismay. I asked one elderly Collach what he thought about his free gift. 'I'm quite happy with pen and paper' he replied. So am I! It's all a far cry from the old hurricane lamp at Port na Luing 40 years ago!

Doreen and I are no longer up to driving very far and we now have to rely on the family to help us get to Coll. My legs let me down at the most inappropriate moments, but, infirm as we are, we still enjoy nothing better than sitting at Port na Luing, watching the ever changing seascape, entertaining friends and just soaking up the atmosphere . . . there may have been many changes on Coll in the years we have known it, but some things will never change!